The Real Life Investing Guide

The Real Life Investing Guide

Kenan Pollack
Eric Heighberger

McGraw-Hill

New York San Francisco Washington, D.C. Auckland Bogota
Caracas Lisbon London Madrid Mexico City Milan
Montreal New Delhi San Juan Singapore
Sydney Tokyo Toronto

Library of Congress Cataloging-in-Publication Data

Pollack, Kenan.
    The real life investing guide / Kenan Pollack, Eric Heighberger.
       p.   cm.
    Includes index.
    ISBN 0-07-050319-2 (alk. paper)
    1. Investments—Handbooks, manuals, etc. I. Heighberger, Eric.
II. Title.
HG4527.P65   1998
332.67′8—dc21
                                    97-30507
                                        CIP

McGraw-Hill

A Division of The McGraw·Hill Companies

   3 4 5 6 7 8 9 0 DOC/DOC 9 0 2 1 0 9 8

ISBN 0-07-050319-2

The sponsoring editor for this book was Mary Glenn, the editing supervisor was Patricia V. Amoroso, and the production supervisor was Sherri Souffrance.

Printed and bound by R. R. Donnelley & Sons Company.

This publication is designed to provide accurate and authoritative information in regard to the subject matter covered. It is sold with the understanding that the publisher is not engaged in rendering legal, accounting, or other professional service. If legal advice or other expert assistance is required, the services of a competent professional person should be sought.
                —*From a declaration of principles jointly adopted by a committee of the American Bar Association and a committee of publishers.*

This book is printed on recycled, acid-free paper containing a minimum of 50% recycled, de-inked fiber.

McGraw-Hill books are available at special quantity discounts to use as premiums and sales promotions, or for use in corporate training programs. For more information, please write to the Director of Special Sales, McGraw-Hill, 11 West 19th Street, New York, NY 10011. Or contact your local bookstore.

Contents

Music, and Investing, for the Masses

"The time to rise has been engaged." With those words, R.E.M. opened their fifth album, *Document*. The tune from which those lyrics are lifted, "Finest Worksong," was not written about personal finance or Wall Street investing, but for a legion of young individuals facing the prospect of an uncertain future, no truer words were ever spoken. Or sung.

That said, it's not coincidental that we decided to use the story of R.E.M., the highly influential folk-rock band from Athens, Georgia, to open our first chapter about the basics of investing. The group's story is not only an interesting chapter in the history of alternative music in the early 1980s, but it's analogous to that of a small company that succeeds and grows over time, rewarding its early supporters. With pop culture tales like that, and other nonfinance touches, we hope to give investing an attractive element for those perhaps not steeped in the world of stocks, bonds, and mutual funds. If that description sounds familiar, then read on.

For all too long, investing has been the domain of the older, more established and well-to-do. In days past, the younger members of society seemed neither to care about investing nor find its concepts and terminology easy to swallow. With little concern about the financial future, there was neither the impetus nor feasibility to get started in the world of Wall Street. These days, both the playing field and the rules have changed. The result is a whole new breed of investor.

What's the catalyst behind this youth-investing movement? For one, there's the future. While our parents slept soundly, believing in company pension plans or robust entitlement programs, our generation has learned to think otherwise. Much-touted surveys, such as those from the twenty-something advocacy group Third Millennium, note that today's youth have more faith in the existence of UFOs than Social Security being around by the time they retire. That shouldn't come as a huge surprise, since by some estimates, Social Security could go belly up by 2029. Other polls note that young Americans think the soap opera *General Hospital* will outlast the federal Medicare program. Hyped polls aside, the real issue is that this younger generation realizes that they alone will be responsible for themselves and their finances. More important, they are starting to do something about it.

The shifts on Wall Street too have been nothing less than tectonic. With the explosion of mutual funds and discount brokers–even stock plans that allow individuals to open accounts cheaply and directly through the company–beginning investors can tap into the stock market's historic growth with just $50. Sources of financial information have blossomed, too. With loads of magazines and journals, the Internet, and the World Wide Web, access to a bounty of financial information, ranging from real-time stock quotes to comprehensive company profiles, has never been easier. In some ways this trend is remarkable. Much of this exclusive data was once the province of high-profile investment houses and their exclusive clients. It's now become the territory of the masses. Like kindling to the flame, this future uncertainty, coupled with the lowered barriers to entry–unprecedented in the market's history–have helped fuel this generation's embrace of investing.

Articles in financial publications, from *The Wall Street Journal* to *Fortune*, and surveys such as one from the Securities Industry Association have noted that thousands of younger Americans have already jumped aboard the investing bandwagon. A 1997 survey conducted for NASDAQ, a computer-based stock trading network, found that already a majority of investors, some 55 percent, are under the age of 50. Many have ventured into stocks, others into bonds, and legions more into mutual funds. Some say it's for their long-term goals like buying a home or retirement, even their kids' college tuition. (Not bad for individuals who not that long ago left the main quad themselves.) Others point to short-term goals like graduate school a few years down the road, or a new car. After all, when the basic savings account barely keeps pace with inflation, this generation has learned that the market is the more important place to put its hard-earned dollars.

While many have already started investing, there are millions more who are still waiting in the wings. Whether they simply lack the push or discipline to get started, they are missing out on a historic time. They are not to blame. After all, investing doesn't carry the same appeal as a skiing weekend or camping trip. Never mind that too many sources of financial information are targeted toward users twice their age. It is for this group of young would-be investors that we created *The Real Life Investing Guide.* Dedicated to the proposition that investing *can* be interesting as well as beneficial, *The Real Life Investing Guide* provides the reader with the basics of investing in a compelling way that goes beyond stock tables and balance sheets. One recurring theme used throughout the book, for instance, is music. We opted for that approach because the parallels to the investing world are striking. And there are definitely those people—and we're the first to admit it—who have a much greater interest in reading up on U2 than 401(k)s.

The Real Life Investing Guide is broken into five major chapters: "Investing 101: Just the Facts", "Maximum Securities: Stocks and Bonds," "From Mosh Pits to Mutual Funds," "Grad School, Travel, or New Wheels: Saving for Short-Term Goals," and "Plaid Trousers in the Sun: Investing for Retirement." These sections can be read individually or in any sequence, depending on the reader's needs. For those beginning from scratch, we suggest starting with Chapter 1. From there, the book goes from the general (What is risk? What is a mutual fund?) to the specific (What are the tax issues to consider with an IRA?). Incidentally, the largest chapter in the book is on stocks and bonds. This is not because we suggest a stock-only investment strategy, but rather that these securities will most likely, directly or indirectly, constitute a bulk of a long-term portfolio holding. We strongly recommend that readers start learning now about what they are and how they work.

If you're looking for some hot stocks, let us save you some time: You *won't* find that information here. You also won't score any get-rich-quick investing suggestions. What you *will* find is information geared directly toward the needs of beginning investors. For example, on page 92 is a list of 10 highly-rated mutual fund companies that let you open an account with just $50. On page 18 is an expert's opinion on handling credit card debt and investing. In addition, there are charts, graphs, and profiles of young people who are already investing. There are also quirky statistics (How many crayons does the typical 10-year-old use? Answer on page 62) to make this anything but a typical text-only financial guide. You can also find more interactive features and additional information on our web site at http://www.rlig.com.

Total personal finance involves comprehensive, smart money management and fiscal responsibility. This book is geared toward one element of that: investing. By using this resource, we hope that current and future investors will be able to either pursue additional information at their own pace or seek the help of professionals in the field. Either way, we would like the reader to take away from *The Real Life Investing Guide* a better understanding of how the world of investing works and pin down the basics to get started. In the case of working with professionals, we hope the book helps you to ask the right questions and simply be informed to create a long-term investment strategy for the years ahead. For when it comes to graduating to more advanced sources of information, there is simply no lack of places to turn: bookstores, newsstands, television, the Internet .... Our interest is providing a helpful–and enticing–first step in that direction.

Investing can be cool, but we're the first to admit that no one in his or her youth who wasn't an investing prodigy at age six wants to spend a lot of free time immersed in the topic. After all, there are great concerts to see and new CDs to hear. It's our firm belief that no one need sacrifice the youth associated with in-line skating or mosh pits just yet for the responsibility implied with owning a mutual fund.

In fact, we hope you can manage both.

Kenan Pollack
Eric Heighberger
Washington, DC
1997

 # Acknowledgments

Producing a book, we quickly learned, requires nothing short of a team effort and there are dozens of people we would like to thank for their help, interest, and encouragement. To these countless masses, we'd like to extend a blanket "thank you" for your help, encouragement, and quiet toleration (i.e., harassing email) of our "we have to do book work" excuses over the past many months.

There are a few people, however, we would like to list individually for helping to make this publication possible. They date back to the early days when the book was just a notion, way back in that cramped—but always clean, mind you—Washington, DC, apartment. They are:

Our agent, Howard Yoon, with Lichtman, Trister, Singer & Ross, who faithfully pushed our idea from the outset and worked with us along the way. Your management, criticisms, and, of course, your humor has been invaluable during this two-plus year publishing pilgrimage.

Marcia Simpkins, Vice President of Wheat First Butcher Singer in Washington, DC, and investment advisor Robert Levitt in Boca Raton, FL, for reading our manuscript and providing insightful, expert comments that made the text a more accurate and better read for younger and older investors alike.

Mary Brophy Marcus and Daniel Yoo, for bringing the pages that follow alive with charts, graphs, icons, and the like. Your dedicated work and creative eye lifted our ideas to the next level, and for that we are grateful.

The editors, past and present, of McGraw-Hill, who turned this vision of a twentysomething investment guide from a basic proposal to a real (life) book. In particular we would like to extend our gratitude to Dave Conti, Alyson Arias, and, of course, Mary Glenn for their interest in the book and help along the way. We are pleased and honored to have worked with each one of you over the past two years.

To each and every one of you, thanks again for all your help.

And now our feature presentation...

Kenan Pollack
Eric Heighberger
Washington, DC

The Real Life Investing Guide

Investing 101: Just the Facts

There's only one way of life and that's your own.
—The Levellers*

When Bands Are Like Companies

Step back to the year 1981. Ronald Reagan has just taken office in January. Two months later, he will be wounded during an assassination attempt by John Hinckley, Jr. outside the Washington Hilton in the nation's capital. NASA's Space Shuttle program will take its maiden orbital flight when Columbia is launched in April. The Rubik's Cube is all the rage, and the hot new TV show is *The Greatest American Hero*. That same year a new band named R.E.M., formed a year earlier in Athens, Georgia, releases a couple of seven-inch singles, including "Radio Free Europe" on the tiny hometown Hib-Tone label. Suppose you were a big music fan back then and happened to buy the two singles on the advice of a friend for three dollars each.

The following year R.E.M. signs with the college-band label IRS Records and releases its first mini-album, *Chronic Town*, to wide critical acclaim. In 1983, when the band puts out its first full-length album, *Murmur*, the music critics and college radio stations give it a major thumbs up. The song "Radio Free Europe," previously released on *Chronic Town* and also on *Murmur*, becomes an instant classic.

The next year the band comes out with *Reckoning* and the year after that *Fables of the Reconstruction*. Both albums increase the popularity and following of the band nationwide. By the time R.E.M.'s fourth album, *Life's Rich Pageant*, comes out in 1986, the group is only heading in one direction: up. In a 1987 cover story, *Rolling Stone* magazine dubs R.E.M. America's best band. Their next album, *Document*, contains the band's first big hit, "The One I Love," and it helps take the album to the top 10 charts. At this point the band, once denizens of small clubs and theaters, is selling out major arenas everywhere. There's little doubt: R.E.M. is huge.

By 1987, six years after you purchased those singles for just a few dollars, their value has exploded. Used record stores are offering up to 10 times what you paid for them back in 1981. Two factors combined to boost the value of what were simply singles from a no-name band on a no-name label. First, the band's incredible success prompted huge demand for virtually everything about them from old T-shirts and posters to bootleg recordings. Second, the introduction of the CD–and the subsequent decline in the production of vinyl albums–further boosted the value of these hard-to-find items to collector's status. By the time you eventually sell the Hib-Tone singles at a used record store–after trading in your turntable for a CD player, the three dollars you *invested* in the singles fetches a $30 price tag, a 500 percent profit over the original purchase price. Not bad, you note, as you quietly thank Michael, Peter, Mike, and Bill.

The point here isn't about the sucess of R.E.M., the music Mecca that was Athens, Georgia or even whether early R.E.M. fans are bitter that the band got so popular. It's simply a story about harnessing the growth and power of a small group that makes it big. Indeed, replace the name R.E.M. with that of a company like Microsoft or Intel, and swap that 1981 small Hib-Tone label record purchase with the procurement of company stock and the parallels to the world of investing become clearer.

Music aside, instances of investing abound in everyday life and may date back to our childhood. For instance, did you ever collect and trade baseball cards? Or perhaps obscure Barbie dolls, like that limited-edition Disco Dater Barbie? Or old *Star Wars* figures? The flashback session ends here, but the investing parallels do not. Many of the most basic and fundamental investing concepts explained in the pages ahead follow the same lines as those action figures and trading cards. Along the way you may encounter descriptions of terms new to you. But as for the absolute fundamental: putting money into something and watching it grow, you're probably already a proponent of that practice. If so, congratulations and welcome to the world of investing.

Investing: What's Up?

Thinking about investing, might trigger memories of the ultraslick finance mogul Gordon Gekko brokering massive stock transactions in the movie *Wall Street*. Other images come from investment firm television commercials showing a retired couple enjoying their golden years. The voice-over lets us know they're financially carefree now because they were wise enough to start and maintain their investing program with the professional advice of this particular firm. While such visual metaphors

> **Investing:** Putting money into securities such as stocks, bonds, or mutual funds with the hope that it will grow in value.

give investing a human side, they unfortunately give it the wrong one for a new and younger group of investors. The customary definition for investing is that it is the process of putting money into instruments (stocks, bonds, or mutual funds and other securities, to be described later) where it is expected to increase in value. The problem with both of these images is that they convey the *opposite* of what young investors should be doing, waiting until they're rich or older to get started with the process. So instead, when thinking about the concept of investing, focus on that young music fan who bought the early R.E.M. records or collected a Baltimore Oriole's Cal Ripken rookie card. It's a lot more interesting, and it probably holds more personal meaning.

PROFILE
Hugh Wooden, 27
St. Louis, MO

When he's planning to run a marathon, exercise enthusiast Hugh Wooden has learned that training early and perserverance always pay off. When it comes to investing for the future, he's realized much the same thing. Hugh, a first-year MBA student at Washington University in St. Louis, started investing 15 percent of his salary toward his retirement account in 1993. His company, then a litigation consulting firm, matched his contributions 50 cents on the dollar for the first 3 percent of his salary. By 1997, that investment was valued at over $19,000. In addition to this plan, Hugh has also started investing in mutual funds on his own, including the T. Rowe Price New Asia fund and the Montgomery Global Communications Fund. The total of both investments is over $11,000—achieved with average monthly contributions of just $200. Hugh hopes to apply this savings toward an early retirement and pursue his other interests; golf, biking, and travel. His only wish is that he had started saving as a teenager.

Why Should I Care?

Perhaps the most basic, easy-to-answer question is: Why should I invest in the first place? Couldn't I just save money in the bank or a coffee can stored under the futon for some future expense like graduate school, a down payment on a car, or a trip to the islands? Maybe the easiest way to think forward is to look back.

Think for a second about the average expenditure for a new car back in 1981. (The answer: $8910.) In 1996 it was $18,565. It doesn't take a finance major to realize that the prices of many things have gone up over the years (in the case of that car, 106 percent). Such increases in price are all or partially related to inflation.

Inflation is the rate at which prices for everything, from a loaf of bread to a new car, increase over time. And increase they do. When grandpa fumes about the price of a new pair of plaid trousers these days, compared to the pair he bought back in the good-old days, he's serving double duty as a grumpy old man

Future (Price) Shock

Forget the Ph.D. in economics. To determine if the prices of goods and services increase over time, go to any store today and compare costs from years ago. Inflation–the rate at which the cost of goods or services increases over time–is the culprit. The Bureau of Labor Statistics in Washington tracks such price increases with something called the CPI, or Consumer Price Index, which is a price composite of goods and services. The following is a sampling of price changes of specific goods between 1986 and the end of 1996, unless otherwise noted.

Product/Service	Price Change from 1986 through 1996
Gasoline, unleaded regular (thru Nov. 1996)	+4 percent
Women's Dresses	+6 percent
Sporting goods	+17 percent
Women's coats and jackets	+23 percent
Sofas	+38 percent
Sirloin steak	+39 percent
Rent, residential	+42 percent
Cheese	+45 percent
Fish and seafood	+53 percent
Cereal	+54 percent
Airline fares (1989 to 1996)	+60 percent
Eggs	+60 percent
Apples	+66 percent
Automobile insurance	+94 percent
Tobaccco and smoking products	+94 percent
Prescription drugs	+97 percent
College tuition	+128 percent

Source: U.S. Department of Labor, Bureau of Labor Statistics

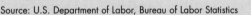

and as an inflation barometer. That same increase is often true when considering the cost of college, clothing, coffee, or any other household product or service. You name it.

So how does all this affect your ability to save for something like a mountain bike in the future, and why doesn't a coffee can work? Good question. Suppose you spot a new mountain bike selling for $600. You don't have that kind of money (and you opt not to do the credit card thing)... so you decide to save $50 a month in a coffee can. If you diligently sock away that amount every month, you'll have your $600 in one year's time. But before planning what trails to hit with the new bike a year from now, consider a little history. For most of this century, the rate of inflation, which is measured as a yearly percentage, has averaged about 3 percent per year. That means every year the prices of most goods and services increase about 3 percent on average. And while some goods may actually drop in price, like VCRs, CD players, or laptop computers (thanks to technological and manufacturing advances), other expenses, like college tuition and health care costs, have grown faster than the average inflation rate. In short, if this historic trend continues, that $600 mountain bike will cost $618 by the following year, and you would fall short in your savings by $18. That's not a big deal, but consider what would happen if that expense were, say, a new $15,000 car ($450 increase), an MBA degree costing $40,000 between tuition and expenses ($1200 increase) or a new $200,000 house ($6000 increase)! The actual price increase could be massive, and even more, worrisome. That 3 percent rate could conceivably jump, in any given year, to a higher rate. In 1980 inflation was 13.5 percent. At that rate, that $600 mountain bike would be approaching $700 the following year.

Compounding:
The process of growth building upon growth in an investment. The result is increased gains on the investment over time.

To guard against those price increases, people often turn to investing. This provides them a way to make more money than they lose through inflation, a process known as "outpacing inflation." So in the future, when you decide to buy a new set of wheels or make a down payment on a new house, it is extremely important that the value of your savings be more, not less, than when you started.

Young and Restless: The Need to Start Now

If the everyday stress of your job, school, or family is bad enough, then worrying about saving for the future, particularly something such as retirement, seems downright laughable. But not dealing with the issue now may mean trouble down the road, and while it may seem difficult to get started at this point, it's at least important to learn the basics. For those who can start now, while young, there's a great chance to take advantage of the most important element in the investing world—for free. It's called time.

Time

In the world of investing, time works wonders. Suppose the $1000 that was initially headed for the coffee can was diverted toward an investment where the money could grow at an average of, say, 12 percent annually. Not

The Compounding Engine—Starting Early Is the Key

Even if you don't have much money, it's better to start investing sooner rather than later because of the magic of compounding. As the chart on page 8 shows, investing earlier with less money provides a bigger payoff in the long run than waiting to invest with more. For example, suppose Investor A (let's call her Lisa) invested $2000 a year starting at age 25. After 10 years she stopped adding more money, but the $20,000 she had invested to date was allowed to grow and compound. The same year she stopped investing, Investor B (Bart) started putting away $2000 annually and continued to do so for 30 years, contributing a total of $60,000. As evident in the graph, even though Lisa put away only one-third the amount that Bart did, she would have made $556,197.07, nearly 60 percent more than his $328,988.05 (based on an investment earning 10 percent annually). The reason: Her original investment of $20,000—although much less than Bart's $60,000—had more time to compound. That's the advantage of starting to save while you're young.

including taxes or other expenses, at the end of the first year, that $1000 would be worth $1120 ($1000 x .12 = $120). Easy enough. But consider year two. The beginning balance going into that year is no longer $1000 but $1120. That means that $1120 would now be earning a 12 percent return. At the end of year two the total balance would be $1254.40, $14.40 extra growth over the $120 the year before. That may not seem like a big difference now, but consider what that would mean 10,

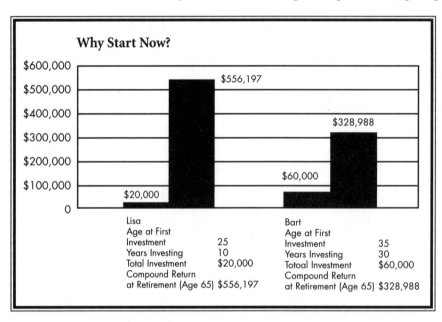

Why Start Now?

	Lisa	Bart
Age at First Investment	25	35
Years Investing	10	30
Total Investment	$20,000	$60,000
Compound Return at Retirement (Age 65)	$556,197	$328,988

Chart values: $20,000; $556,197; $60,000; $328,988

20 or as much as 40 years down the road. In fact, this notion, known as *compounding*, or growth building upon growth, is an extremely powerful engine that can drive a small investment into a big one over time, even if we're only talking about modest-sized investments.

More Compounding Stats

For $24 and some beads, Native Americans, in what is now New York, sold Manhattan Island to Dutch settlers back in 1626. Not a lot of money, obviously. However, if the Native Americans had invested that money starting then and earned an average rate of return of just 6 percent annually, by the year 1997, that $24 would be worth a staggering $58,706,644,075 (that is almost $59 billion).

The Very Basics

Risk Is First

Chances are one of your perceptions of investing is that it's risky and that you could squander all your money, like at a craps table or poker game. Well, yes and no. Yes, investing does involve risk. Headlines may blare "Stock Market Crash" or "Economic Recession Looming," but in many ways it's much the same as driving a car or playing sports. Risk is going to be there, and you learn to deal with it. But unlike some powerless entity, helpless to influence your surroundings, when you begin investing, you can control and deal with risk responsibly if you understand what it means and how it works.

One finance handbook defines risk as the "measurable possibility of losing or not gaining value. Risk is differentiated from uncertainty, which is not measurable..." In English, it's a calculated gamble with money. For instance, *Let's Make a Deal*'s coy host, Monty Hall, would pose the classic decision question to his costumed guests, "You can take this $500 I have in my hand or trade it for whatever is behind curtain number three." It's an intriguing and often disconcerting position: Stick with a known sum, or risk it for the possibility of more. There is less risk with the guest taking what they know they have, $500, but in doing so, they lose the option of hitting it big with the elusive curtain number three (perhaps a new car, or that ever-serviceable pack mule).

Risk: *Uncertainty as to whether an investment choice will perform as expected, particularly owing to factors beyond one's control (in other words, the odds an investment will lose money).*

Investing is not a game show, but the decisions and the risks are clearly there. When investing, risk is something that can never be avoided entirely if you want to achieve long-term growth with your money. Moreover, risk needs to be embraced at times, particularly for those looking 10 or 20 years down the road for maybe a new house or condo. Why? Because to make more money through investing, you have to assume more risk. Think of it in terms of slot machines at a casino. If you want to increase your chances of winning a larger prize, you have to gamble more. That means bypassing the nickel machines for the quarter, half-dollar, one dollar, or even five-dollar one-armed bandits. The risk of losing more money increases with those higher-charging games, but the chance of a bigger payoff increases as well. Consider the jackpot a $5 slot would pay versus a nickle slot. But also consider how much you might lose at that $5 machine, going for the glory. So barring some impeccable luck and triple 7's at the nickel slots (and, yes, some grandmothers pull that off), the real chance of increasing your return comes from increasing your risk of loss as well.

PROFILE

Steve Hagerty, 28, and Lisa Altenbernd, 30, Baltimore, Maryland

Steve Hagerty and Lisa Altenbernd were married in 1995 after both received graduate degrees from Syracuse University. They live only a few minutes walk from Camden Yards, home of the Baltimore Orioles, in a house they purchased in 1996. Steve currently works as a consultant in the Office of Government Services at Price Waterhouse, although he one day hopes to start and run his own company. Lisa is a research associate at Macro International, a human services research firm. Both save for retirement diligently through 401(k) plans (explained in Chapter 5) provided by their companies. Lisa saves 12 percent of her salary in the plan each month; Steve puts away15 percent. "We save and invest in order to have the means to purchase things we may want in the future. We try to live on only one salary and save the other," they say. Steve and Lisa achieve that goal by keeping an eye on costs. Some of their methods include shopping with coupons, conserving energy, putting off unnecessary purchases (their Ford Escort, which they affectionately refer to as "The Pony," has topped the 100,000 mile mark), and eating in instead of dining out. Except for the house, they carry no debt. They try to set savings goals for themselves and keep three months' salary in a money market account as a general emergency fund as well as for things such as furniture.

In order to go after bigger returns, the kind that make money grow substantially over time, you have to go with riskier investments. Not doing so, while safer, will only lead to depressed growth in the future. So while the coffee can is virtually risk-free (short of getting stolen), it does nothing in the way of returns. The bank account, by the same token, is also very safe (Deposits up to $100,000 are fully protected by the U.S. government.) But it rarely outpaces inflation. On the other hand, a modest investment in an up-and-coming company, which may be considered a risky investment, could provide attractive returns down the road.

Risk is one of the most important factors to consider when investing. Markets can soar or sink, the economy can churn or sputter, and prices can skyrocket or plummet. That's a given. It's critical to choose an investment option that matches your ability to tolerate risk. And those in finance have created tests to help you gauge your capacity to deal with risk (risk tolerance) or avoid it like spoiled milk (risk aversion). The following quiz should help give you some sense of where you lie on that all-important comfort spectrum. Take a second to pick your answers. At the bottom are point values assigned to those answers, which, when added together, should help you determine if you embrace or avoid risk.

Goals of Investing: Before investing a dime, it's critical to assess just why you want to invest in the first place and how much risk you are willing to assume to meet that goal. A down payment for a new car in two years requires a totally different strategy than saving for retirement in 40. Whichever your goal, it's most important that the investment option match that goal, both in terms of time and your risk tolerance.
For starters, consider these questions:

- *What am I investing for?*
- *How long do I plan to have this money invested?*
- *How much risk am I willing to assume with my invested money?*
- *How much money am I prepared to invest?*

1. Even though the chips and salsa are delicious, you're down $500 in a poker game. How much more would you bet to get the $500 back?
   a. More than $500.
   b. $500.
   c. $250.
   d. Nothing, stick with the nachos and eat your losses now.

2. A friend who's good with numbers convinces you to invest $500 in a new hot stock. One year later, the value has risen 40 percent. Would you:
   a. Hold it, hoping for more gains.
   b. Sell it and take your gains now.
   c. Buy more shares, as it could go higher.

3. A month after you put most of your long-term savings in stocks, the market, and your investments drops 30 percent in value. Would you:
   a. Buy more shares after the price drop.
   b. Hold on and wait for the price to come back then sell.
   c. Sell immediately to avoid losing even more.

4. For the past year, you've been busting your rump at a small company. As a thank you gesture, your boss offers you a bonus of $1000 in cash or stock options worth $2000. The cash can be received immediately, but the stock options cannot be redeemed for at least 4 months and during that time the price may sail or plummet. Which would you take:
   a. The $1000 cash bonus
   b. The stock options currently worth $2000

5. You just received a $10,000 inheritance to invest. Would you:
   a. Invest it all at once.
   b. Invest it gradually over time.

Answers:

Question 1:   If you chose A, give yourself 9 point; B, 5 points; C, 3 points; and D, 1 points

Question 2:   If you chose A, give yourself 3 points; B, 1 points; C, 4 points

Question 3:   If you chose A, give yourself 4 points; B, 3 point; C, 1 points

Question 4:   If you chose A, give yourself 1 point; B, 5 points

Question 5:   If you chose A, give yourself 5 points; B, 1 points

Scoring: If your score totaled 6 to 16 points, you may have the leanings of a more conservative investor. Your investment strategies should probably be more stable and predictable. This does not mean you'll be able to avoid risk altogether, but you should be careful in choosing those investments that will limit you worrying all night about possible losses in your portfolio.

If you scored between 17 to 27 points, you're probably willing to take more chances with your money to earn higher returns down the road. While not thrilled with the idea, you may be more comfortable with the idea of short-term losses, that often follow the riskier investments you may be more likely to approach. To you, the extra reward is worth the extra risk.

Hey Buddy, You Have the Time!

All right, you've gauged where you lie on the risk ruler. But here's an additional twist to that equation: time. Time is an extremely important factor in determining what kind of risk to embrace when deciding on investment options. In much the same way that there's a strong association between risk and return, there's a strong association between time, risk, and return. In the simplest terms, an investment may be risky in any given year. If we're talking stocks, for example, the company could have a bad year, or the market could sour. But over time, those price fluctuations in investments tend to smooth out. And historically, or at least for most of this century, that trend has been generally onward and upward. The riskier investments provide the best returns and the safer ones much lower returns.

Investing in small company stocks, (young, start-up companies), for example, is generally a riskier investment than putting money into older, more established companies, since younger firms are more likely not to live up to expectations. But small stocks have also produced an average annual return of 12.6 percent from 1926 to 1996. Also, consider the much safer Treasury Bills, those securities completely guaranteed by the federal government which have returned just 3.7 percent throughout those same years. That's less than one percent over inflation, which averaged 3.1 percent during that time. Those who invested in

Comparison of Investment Returns, 1926-1996

Type of Investment	Compound Annual Return
Small Company Stocks	12.6 percent
Large Company Stocks	10.7 percent
Long-Term Corporate Bonds	5.6 percent
Long-Term Government Bonds	5.1 percent
Treasury Bills	3.7 percent
Inflation	3.1 percent

small company stocks assumed a greater risk than those in Treasury Bills, but they enjoyed a nearly 8.9 percent annual advantage for their risk tolerance and safely outpaced inflation in the process. In a later chapter we'll explore further what kinds of investments to consider for long-term investing.

Short-term investing—for the next five or ten years, for instance—requires a completely different approach to return and risks than longer-term investing. This will also be explored later. Suffice it to say that those looking to pay for a new car in five years or graduate school in three need to carefully consider their options, and should focus on a much shorter investment horizon and on matching their investments to this time frame.

Return

In order to beat inflation and determine whether an investment is making or losing money, it's important to understand how investment performance is measured. One term important to understand is called a return. A return is simply a measurement, usually listed as a percentage figure, that tells whether the value of an investment has

Return: *The profit on an investment like a mutual fund or stock. Returns are usually expressed as an annual percentage rate. For example, $500 that was invested in January earning 10 percent would be worth $550 the following January. The return here is $50 on a $500 investment.*

increased or decreased over a specific period of time. For example, suppose $500 were invested on January 1 in an account that was earning an annual return of 6 percent. Not counting any outside expenses or taxes, by December 31 of that same year, the initial deposit of $500 would be worth $530 ($500 x 6 percent = $30). On the flip side an investment that lost 6 percent would only be worth $470 at year's end. Similarly, if $500 were invested in an account on January 1 of one year, and by December 31 it was worth $550 (not including any outside charges or expenses), then it essentially earned a 10 percent return on investment ($550 - $500 = $50).

The return on a particular investment is determined by this equation:
Return = total profit ÷ amount invested

The Rule of 72

Here's a quick way to gauge how long a particular rate of return will take to double your money. It's called the Rule of 72, and it works like this: Divide 72 by the percentage return you expect to get with a certain investment. For example, a 10 percent return will take 7.2 years (72 ÷ 10 = 7.2). In the same way, an 18 percent return would take four years, and a 36 percent return would take just two.

Returns are often measured on either an annualized or compounded rate. An annualized rate is a way of determining on average what an investment made or lost per year over periods of one or more years. For example, if an investment posted an annual return of 40 percent over five years, that's an average of 8 percent annually, or an 8 percent annualized return. Annualized returns enable you to factor out fluctuations in a given year and provide a longer-term picture of an investment's performance. Unfortunately, it also helps to mask those investments that have wild return swings, such as risky investments that may be up 20 percent one year and down 15 percent the next. If you were to take an annualized return approach, it would show a three-year annualized return of around 5 percent, which sounds almost sluggish and calm.

The other way returns are often measured is called compounded returns. Unlike annualized returns which are averaged over the life of the investment, the compounded rate is the sum of each year's return.

The Jedi of the Return: There's no all-powerful "Force" that controls the return on an investment, just good old-fashioned mathematics. Unfortunately, good old-fashioned mathematics can be deceiving. Returns are usually measured in one of two ways: total returns or annualized returns. Total returns measure an investment's cumulative profitability over a specific period of time, like three, five, or ten years. Annualized returns, on the other hand, are the total compounded returns divided by the number of years being measured. For example, an investment may have a five-year total return of 48 percent. The annualized return over those five years would be 9.6 percent (48 ÷ 5 = 9.6). Although each of these measurements is accurate, they can be misleading. There is no way to measure whether this investment will fluctuate wildly between years (up 20 percent one year, down 15 the next), a major concern to many investors seeking constant, stable returns from their investments. Furthermore, the total returns can appear huge ("total return for the past twenty years 240 percent") but average to a more modest 12 percent return annually. In short, when reviewing investment choices, consult a number of sources like, *Value Line Investment Survey* and *Morningstar*, both of which are described later. And most important, check yearly return figures to see how big the variance really is year to year.

Liquidity

Another important investing concept is liquidity. Liquidity is the speed and ease with which an investment can be converted to cash, presumably in the case of an emergency or merely as a convenience. Cash itself is 100 percent liquid, and every other investment is less liquid, to varying degrees. A savings account is considered to be highly liquid since the money can be withdrawn at virtually any time. This contrasts starkly with an investment in real estate. To get the prin-

Liquidity: A measure of the speed and ease at which an investment can be converted to cash. A savings account, for example, is very liquid in that the money can be withdrawn at virtually any time. Real estate, like a house, is not as liquid. It takes a lot more time and effort to sell a home.

This will not be on the test. The face of investing is changing—literally. In 1997, 47 percent of investors were women versus a percentage of 44 percent for white men. A majority of investors are under the age of 50 (55 percent), and one-half are not college graduates.
Source: Peter Hart Research Associates

cipal investment out of real estate, the owner would first have to put the property on the market and then sell it to a buyer who agreed to purchase it at a mutually agreed upon price. This could take days, months, or years.

It's important to take liquidity into account when determining investment options. For example, as measured before, saving for graduate school in three years requires a different strategy than saving for retirement in 40. Three years from now, when it comes time to write a tuition check, you don't want all your investment cash locked up where it can't be accessed easily (e.g., real estate) or without a penalty (e.g., certificates of deposit, which penalize you for early withdrawal).

In investment speak, liquidity is often used interchangably with the term "marketability." Marketability is defined by the speed and ease with which an investment, such as a stock or bond, may be bought and sold. Liquidity, similarily, refers to that as well,

Expert Corner

Paying off credit card debt versus saving for the future: Which should you do first? First it was the Stone Age. Later is was the Space Age. Now it's the Plastic Age, or more appropriately, the Credit Card Age. With a nation of credit happy consumers arises the all-important question: Which should take the priority, beginning to invest while carrying a sizable credit card balance or paying off that hefty Visa or Mastercard balance first? Gary Bowyer, a Chicago-based, fee-only financial advisor, says nix the credit card debt first. The way he sees it, you're guaranteed of getting a 12 to 21 percent return on your money by paying off the credit card debt first (that's the rate most cards charge users on outstanding balances). That makes sense because even if you're investing and earning, say, 10 percent, you're still losing money by paying nearly double that in finance charges. By paying off the credit card debt first, you're at least saving on the finance charges that, by most measurements, will exceed the returns on investments which are not nearly as certain. In short, ditch and control the short-term debt (i.e. take it easy on the plastic), then go long-term with the investing.

but implies the preservation of capital in the process. In other words, when something liquid, such as a savings account, is converted to cash, a person will normally not lose money in the process. On the other hand, when something marketable, such as a stock or bond is sold, the price may be depressed meaning the owner will receive less in cash than what they originally invested, even though the process by which the security was sold was relatively fast and easy. Given the financial vernacular and the confusion these terms sometimes bring, we will stick with the term liquidity, but note when marketability is the more appropriate description.

What Are My Options?

There are a number of ways to save and invest money for the future. These investments, often referred to as "instruments," can range from simple savings accounts at a local bank to more complicated investments involving the world of Wall Street. But they all serve the same purpose: to protect and preserve money (capital) and make it grow. Although each instrument will be explained in greater detail in subsequent chapters, here is a brief description of several of these instru-

---

What are the odds?

If you're considering bagging the investment lesson now because you'd rather sink your time and cash into lottery picks, good luck, you'll need it. Consider the chance of each of these events happening:

• Drawing a pair in poker	4 to 3
• Getting married	3 in 4 (lifetime)
• Cohabiting before marriage	9 in 20
• Having quadruplets	1 in 900,000
• Life on earth being destroyed by a meteorite (over 50-year period)	1 in 1,200,000
• Being killed by a lightning bolt (over one year period)	1 in 3,400,000
• Winning the Powerball lottery jackpot (single winner)	1 in 54,000,000

Source: Excerpts from "Odds and Statistics", as specified from *Numbers: How Many, How Far, How Long, How Much* by Andrea Sutcliffe. Copyright © 1996 by The Stonesong Press, Inc. Reprinted by permission of HarperCollins Publishers, Inc.

---

ments to provide you with a general idea of some of your options. This is by no means a complete list. Rather, it's a collection of those investments that we feel make the most sense for beginners. Once you feel comfortable with these options, there is a more diverse, complex, and advanced world of investing to be explored.

Savings Options

Unlike investing, the goal of savings options is purely to protect the value of the investment from losing money. That means these options must be extremely safe. The flip side of that safety means that savings plans do not offer the individual significant potential for returns. Often, it's only enough to keep up with or barely outpace inflation. The individual should consider savings for short-term financial needs and not for long-term goals, like building a nest-egg for retirement. Briefly described below, each of these options is further explained in Chapter 4.

Savings Account

For many people in their 20s and 30s, savings accounts were the earliest experience with money management and financial institutions. Opened at a bank, savings and loan or credit union, these accounts allow money to be deposited where it will earn interest at a rate set by the market. Savings accounts typically do not pay strong returns, but they are easy to set up and the money can be withdrawn at any time without penalty. Individuals may open a savings account in conjunction with a checking account to provide protection against overdrafts (i.e., bouncing checks).

Liquidity: **High**
Funds from these accounts can be withdrawn at virtually any time.

Risk: **Low**
Savings accounts are insured by the U.S. government (FDIC)for up to $100,000.

Return: **Low**

Interest rates are low, generally at or below the rate of inflation, which means that these accounts are only good for short-term savings.

U.S. Savings Bonds

The odds of having received a U.S. (EE) savings bond from a grandparent as a gift are pretty high. These bonds, issued by the U.S. government, can be purchased at banks and other institutions. You buy them at a discounted price (a $50 bond may sell for $25 dollars or so) and are repaid at their full face value at a later date, known as maturity. For example, a U.S. savings bond may mature 5 years from the date of purchase.

Liquidity: **High**

These bonds can be redeemed at any time; however, the owner will not receive the full face value until the maturity date, which may be years away.

<Online Info>

Here's a tip: When surfing the web for beginning investor information, don't type "Investing" on one of the search engines like Infoseek, Yahoo, or Alta Vista. The results will simply be too massive. (For example, Infoseek brought up 540,000 responses). Always tailor your search with very specific terms, or better yet, check out these sites which offer a number of features helpful to those just starting out:

InvestorWeb
http://www.investorweb.com
Helpful beginner information on investment newsletters and frequently asked investment questions.

Investor Guide
http://www.investorguide.com
Although some of the content is for more advanced investors, there are lots of pages on starter information for those just learning the ropes.

Looking for links? Try:
Financial Web
http://www.finweb.com
Talk about a linkfest. This site's primary objective "is to list Internet resources providing substantive information concerning economics and finance-related topics." That's for sure.

Invest-O-Rama
http://www.investorama.com/
More good links than you care to count on everything, including mutual funds, investment bulletin boards, and usenet groups and general personal finance sites.
</Online Info>

Risk: **Low**

There is little risk of not receiving the full value of these bonds, because as the name suggests they are backed by the full faith and credit of the U.S. government and its taxing power.

Return: **Historically low**

Currently around 5 percent.

Money Market Account

Sophisticated in name, money market accounts are like savings accounts except that they often require a higher minimum balance to open. The money in one of these accounts is invested into quick-maturity securities like some government bonds. The interest made off of these investments is credited to the individual's account. Money market accounts may allow check-writing privileges. However these checks must often be a minimum amount, and you are only allowed to write a certain number of checks per month. The big benefit is that they tend to offer higher interest rates than their savings account companions.

Liquidity: **High**

Money can be withdrawn from the account at any time.

Risk: **Low**

Bank-based money market accounts are federally insured, like savings accounts, against loss.

Return: **Historically low**

Currently around 5 percent, but often higher than savings accounts.

Certificates of Deposit (CD)

Not to be confused with the better-known musical abbreviation, these CDs are purchased through banks or other financial institutions. An individual puts up a sum of money, maybe $500 or $1000, to buy a CD that pays a certain rate of interest and has a certain date of maturity. After the CD is purchased, the individual waits until it matures, at which time he or she is repaid the original amount plus interest that the CD has earned over that time. CDs are very safe in that the funds are protected, but an individual who wishes to cash in before the maturity date pays a stiff penalty for early withdrawal. Interest rates vary on CDs, but in general, the longer the date until maturity, the higher the rate of return on the certificate.

Liquidity: **Low**
If CDs are cashed in before maturity, you pay a substantial penalty for early withdrawal.

Risk: **Low**
Banks CDs are federally insured against loss.

Return: **Historically low**
Currently, CDs average around 5 percent. That rate increases with the longer maturity dates.

Investment Options

As noted, savings plans make sense for short-term goals or emergency cash funds. For financial goals further down the road, however, it's wise to invest funds instead. Investing entails  greater risk, in other words, the chance of losing some or all of your money. Investments are areas, however, where the chance for higher returns is much greater. For long-term investment strategies, this is the category to explore.

Stocks

A stock represents partial ownership in a corporation like General Motors, Coca-Cola, or Disney. Companies issue stock as a way of raising money to fund their operations or expansion. Individuals buy these shares in the hope of making money. Shareholders can profit from investing in two ways. The first is when the company that issues the stock pays shareholders a portion of its profits, called dividends. The second way is when the share price of the stock increases—for any number of reasons—in the market, or stock exchange, where it is traded and is then sold for that higher price.

Liquidity: **High (marketability)**
Stocks can be sold at virtually any time during trading hours, but the share prices are continually changing, which means an individual may end up selling at a lower than desired price.

Risk: **Varies**
Overall, individual stocks are considered risky, in that any number of factors both within and outside the control of the company can depress the price. Thousands of companies, ranging from dinky start-ups to huge century-old multinational corporations, issue stock. Many kinds of issues affect the risk level of a stock. For example, will the firm still be in business come tomorrow?

Return: **Low to high**
Historically, stocks have ranked as the highest returning investments in the industry. Some stocks make money for their shareholders through hefty dividends. Others grow in price over the years, allowing investors to sell for a nice profit. On average, stocks have returned between 10 to 12 percent annually for most of this century, though specific stocks have had higher, lower, or even negative returns.

Bonds

Unlike a stock, which represents partial ownership in the company, purchasing a bond is like giving a loan to a friend. At some point down the road, he or she will return not only the amount you lent, but interest payments as well. With bonds, it's not friends who take the money, but companies or governments, often in increments of $1000. These firms and the government pay out interest on these bonds as a kind of thank you for letting them borrow your money. The interest rate is determined by many factors, including how long the bond was issued for, how stable the issuing firm is (i.e., will they be around years from now to pay it back?), and what the current market interest rates are.

Liquidity: **Low** (if held to maturity) to high (can be traded at anytime, but maturity may be years away)
Bonds generally are held to maturity, which can be weeks, months, years, even decades. The U.S. Government issues 30-year bonds, for example.

Risk: **Low to high**
There are two kinds of risk associated with bonds: interest rate risk and credit risk (both are explained in Chapter 2). Briefly, interest rate risk is a danger that a bond's rate of return will fall below what the rest of the market is paying, and an individual will be stuck holding a less-than-wonderful investment for many years. The second risk, credit risk, is that the organization or government will default on, or not pay, the interest payments on the bond or on the principal come maturity.

Return: **Low to medium**
Can average around 5 percent, but that value is heavily dictated by the market rates, how long the bond was issued for and the creditworthiness of the group issuing the bond. The longer the bond has until maturity and the less stable the firm issuing it, the higher the rate of return will be–to attract investors.

Mutual Funds

Mutual funds are investment companies that pool the money of many individuals and invest it in stocks, bonds, and other securities under the guidance of a professional manager. These funds are an extremely popular investment choice for many people in their 20s and 30s–for several reasons. Some allow investors to get started with just $50. They are very low maintenance. And, most important, they allow diversification, or spreading the risk, with the investor's money. That's because unlike ownership directly in a single stock or bond, mutual fund shareholders may be invested in tens, hundreds, even thousands of stocks and bonds. A price drop in one stock will not hurt the portfolio as a whole as much as it would if that were the sole stock an individual held. Shareholders make money through dividends (when stocks held by the mutual fund declare dividends, it goes to the mutual fund shareholder) and when the price of a share, called the Net Asset Value, of a fund increases (this happens when the value of the fund's portfolio goes up).

Liquidity: High

Investors may sell their shares at any time through the mutual fund company.

Risk: Low to high

Mutual funds are divided into different categories, based upon the goals or objectives of the fund. These objectives often dictate the riskiness of the fund.

Return: Low to high

Like any risk-versus-reward correlation, the real return on a mutual fund depends on its objective. Usually the higher risk funds have the greater returns. They also carry the higher risk of loss.

U.S. Treasury Securities

Treasury Securities are different types of investments, like short-term bills and long-term bonds, that are issued by the Treasury Department and federal agencies. Uncle Sam issues these bonds to finance government operations and to finance the federal deficit.

Liquidity: **High**

Although maturity dates may vary, these securities can usually be sold on the market at any time.

Risk: **Low**

U.S. Treasury securities are backed by the full faith and credit of the federal government.

Return: **Historically low**

Investors pay a price for the virtual safety guarantee on these investments: lower returns than corporate bond issuers. Although the return will vary, currently the average is around 6 percent.

Financial journals and magazines to check out:

As with any subject, when it comes to investing, it pays to be informed. One painless and interesting way to learn the material is by reading, even occasionally, some of the financial journals and newspapers that track the personal finance and investing industry. Here's a sampling of some of the better ones to check out:

Barrons (weekly) 800-328-6800 *http://www.barrons.com/*
A thick, tabloid-sized journal that focuses on the past week's results on Wall Street, including stock roundups and predictions. Lengthy stories on many financial items.

Business Week (weekly) 800-635-1200 *http://www.businessweek.com/*
A lively read, even for the nonbusiness obsessed reader. Of particular interest are the annual Mutual Funds Guide and Where to Invest issues.

Forbes (monthly) 800-888-9896 *http://www.forbes.com/*
Yes, as in 1996 GOP Presidential candidate Steve Forbes (his dad, Malcolm, started the magazine). Coverage in general is business stories, but Forbes covers investment topics too.

Fortune (monthly) 800-621-8000 *http://pathfinder.com/fortune/*
Creators of the legendary Fortune 500 list, this monthly focuses on general business stories and personality profiles, but also puts out an interesting annual investor's guide.

Kiplinger's Personal Finance (monthly) 800-544-0155 *http://www.kiplinger.com/*
Kiplinger's features investment strategies and other consumer journalism pieces like car rankings and scam alerts. Occasionally, it runs pieces geared specifically to the beginning investor.

Money (monthly) 800-633-9970 *http://pathfinder.com/money/*
A well-written general personal finance magazine, but with an obvious spin toward older, "Boomer" investors. There are, however, stories aimed at the twentysomething market.

P.O.V. (monthly) 800-768-6247 *http://www.povmag.com*
Slanted toward the twentysomething men's market, this monthly runs a strong stable of investing and personal finance stories in each issue.

Smart Money (monthly) 800-444-4204
Put out by *The Wall Street Journal*, this monthly often runs a variety of stories, ranging from investment ideas to general personal finance, including insurance and taxes.

U.S. News & World Report (weekly) 800-950-6365 *http://www.usnews.com*
The magazine's "News You Can Use" section covers a variety of investment and personal finance issues, many applicable to readers in their 20s or 30s. Puts out an annual mutual fund and investment guide too.

The Wall Street Journal (daily) 800-778-0840 *http://www.wsj.com/*
Considered a must-read for all finance professionals. The paper's "Money & Investing" section can be especially interesting for new investors. It's not too technical.

Worth (monthly) 800-777-1851 *http://www.worth.com/*
Athough owned by mutual fund giant Fidelity, this magazine provides articles on all kinds of investments, not just mutual funds.

Q.u.i.c.k. D.o.w.n.l.o.a.d.

- Investing is the process of placing money into a security, such as a stock, bond, or mutual fund, and letting it grow over time.

- Individuals invest their money to offset its loss in value due to inflation, which is the rate at which the prices of goods and services change over time.

- The earlier money is invested, the better. That's because the longer money has to compound, or build growth upon growth, the greater its value can increase. And for young investors, although strapped for cash, time is always free.

- Return is the profitability of an investment over time. It's found by dividing the profit by the total amount of an investment and is typically expressed as a percentage rate.

- Risk is the chance that the value of an investment will be diminished or lost over time due to circumstances or forces beyond your control.

- In the investing world, risk and return go hand in hand. To obtain a higher rate of return on an investment, an investor must increase her or his risk. The lower the risk of an investment, the lower its return.

- Before investing, it is critical to determine your risk tolerance and aversion. Selecting investments that match these personal preferences is important for a number of reasons, including wise money management and a good night's rest.

- There are a number of different investment and savings options that an individual can explore. On the savings front, there are savings accounts, certificates of deposit, and money market accounts. On the investing end, there are corporate stocks, bonds, mutual funds, and Treasury securities.

2 Maximum Securities: Stocks and Bonds

*Here we are in a special place. What are you gonna do here? —The Waterboys**

Mow Money

Overcome by an insatiable entrepreneurial urge one fine April day, you and a couple of friends decide to start a grass-cutting business. Sure, one friends notes, the trade is hard work, and the blazing summer sun can be brutal, but there's a real monetary side to the story as well. After all, in the suburban world, there's always a lawn in need of a cut. And there's nothing wrong with working on the tan while you're at it.

After some initial price calculations, the group realizes it will need approximately $1500 in start-up cash to purchase the equipment and supplies that are needed: mowers, weed-trimmers, bags, and a trailer to haul the stuff around. Other costs include promotional flyers to spread the word around the neighborhood and, of course, fuel.

Since no one member of this three-person outfit has $1500 to his or her name, each agrees to put up $500 and become a one-third owner in the new operation. It's also decided that by growing season's end in October, any money left over after expenses will be divided up between the three if the business decides to call it quits for bigger and better things (or a respite in the world of climate control).

After some marketing summits and sales plans, your group names the company *Lawn and Order*. The name and earnest sales pitch work, as 10 homes sign on initially, with 20 more added to the ranks a few weeks later. Soon, every day is spent cutting grass and bringing in revenue. In turn, the company expands operations into basic landscaping including weed-pulling, hedge-trimming, and edging. With those additional offerings, several more homes sign on and the revenue increases. The three of you each get a weekly paycheck based on the number of hours worked, and the extra cash goes into a savings account for short-term holding and to cover costs.

As the months progress, *Lawn and Order* becomes a more efficient operation (big, time-consuming lawns in the morning before the afternoon heat; faster small lawns later in the day). Revenue continues all the while. By October, the cutting business ends and the company shifts to raking leaves for the month. After all, it's good to have closure on the same lawns you've tended all summer. By the start of November, you and your partners call it quits. Even after covering the paychecks and expenses, the company's savings account has grown to $3000. Divided by three, the founding partners received their $500 back, plus an extra $500 in profits. In just six months, that initial investment of $500 had doubled, a 100 percent return on the investment. Not bad for a summer's work and short introduction to business start-ups, company profits, and the world of stocks.

What Is a Stock?

Similar to the founders who put up the money for a stake in the grass-cutting business, a stock represents a chunk of ownership of a corporation. Corporations issue stock as a way to raise money (capital) to fund the expansion of the business in various ways. In doing so, ownership is handed over to tens, hundreds, or thousands of individuals.

The obvious question on the other end is: Why would investors want to buy stock in the first place? The simple answer is to make money. As partial owners of the company, investors enjoy a number of privileges, including annual reports, free products or services, the ability to vote on the corporation's management from time to time, and most important, a chance to share in the profits of the company.

Stock: *A security that represents partial ownership in a corporation.*

How Stocks Make Money

Stockholders can make money in one of two ways: through (1) dividend earnings or (2) capital appreciation. When a company is successful and makes a profit, known as earnings, the corporation may decide to share some of that money with its stockholders as a "thank you" gesture for purchasing their stock. That payment, which is usually issued every three months, or quarter, is known as a dividend.

Dividend: *Cash profits that are distributed to the shareholders of a corporation or mutual fund. It's usually given out quarterly, and it is taxable.*

There is no absolute rule about what companies pay dividends (they don't have to; in fact, they may even pay out dividends when they do not make a profit just to be consistent), or how much they pay, but a large number of publicly traded companies choose to do this as a way of rewarding their shareholders and as a way of building loyalty. Other firms may add additional freebies for purchasing their stock. Wrigley's, for instance, gives each shareholder 20 free packs of gum every year; 3M distributes free Post-It Note packs to their stock owners.

Shareholders can also make money with stocks when the price per share increases in the stock market. This is known as capital appreciation. The price of a stock may increase for a variety of reasons: The company just announced a very strong earnings report that quarter; a product is introduced that could dominate a market and be very profitable; there are plans to be taken over by another company; or the economy is doing well and most stock market prices seem to be rising. Whatever the reason for the price increase, a shareholder only earns a profit when he or she actually sells the shares at the increased price. This is known as a realized gain. Until that point, the price increase is known as an unrealized gain and is often referred to as a "paper profit." Conversely, if the price were to drop, but the shareholder opted not to sell the shares, this would be known as an "unrealized" or "paper" loss since the shareholder has not actually lost any money yet from the portfolio. On a daily basis, a stockholder can determine the unrealized loss or gain of his or her holdings by comparing the price paid for the stock versus the price at which it closes on a particular day.

> **Capital appreciation:** the rise in value of a security, such as a stock, due to market forces of supply and demand.

Nuts and Bolts

In the world of finance, when a private company (one that does not offer shares to the general populace) decides to issue stock for the first time, the process is known as "going public." This first availability of any given stock to the public is known as an initial public offering, or

IPO, and often can get a lot of press. Firms like Netscape, Pixar, and Boston Chicken went public amid loads of hype, for instance.

When a company goes public, it may offer two different categories of stock: *preferred stock* or *common stock*. There are a couple of important differences. Common stock, as the name implies, is the much more prevalent of the two. Common stock gives investors the right to vote on issues involving the management of the company, unlike preferred stock. Another difference is how dividends are distributed. Preferred stockholders agree to receive their dividends at a fixed rate over time, whereas the common stock dividend may go up or down each quarter, depending on the financial standing of the

Stock It To Me

Look at the value of $1.00 invested into stocks in 1800: $5.6 million now.

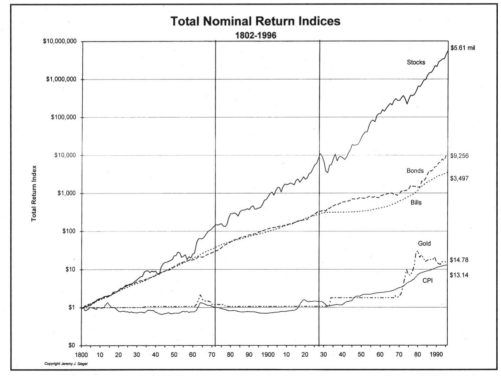

Source: Copyright © Jeremy J. Siegel

company. If a company is doing well financially, it may increase dividends; if times are tough, it could decrease them.

Trading Places

After a company completes the process of going public, the stock of that firm is traded on a stock exchange. A stock exchange is an organized place where stocks are traded between buyers and sellers. On the New York Stock Exchange, located on Wall Street, stocks from nearly 3000 different companies are traded. Trading is done on the exchange "floor," where "buy" and "sell" orders are carried out at circular computer-laden booths. In those booths specialists match up buyers and sellers for a particular stock. Specialists act as mediators between buyers and sellers, adjusting the price of a stock as needed to ensure that necessary transactions get accomplished. However, while the human side of trading is interesting, and makes the financial backdrop on the nightly news, most trades are done electronically–zipped in and out of the exchange via computer. This trading commotion starts every business day at 9:30 in the morning and lasts until 4:00 in the afternoon, New York time. Most of the major corporations, like General Motors, Coca-Cola, and Disney, are traded on the New York Stock Exchange (NYSE).

In order to be listed on a specific exchange, a company must meet certain guidelines including:				
Exchange	**No. Shareholders or shares listed**	**Stock market minimum value**	**Pre-tax earnings**	**Number of stocks listed**
NYSE	1.1 million shares	$18 million	$2.5 million per year	3000
AMEX	500,000 shares	$3 million	$750,000 in last year (or 2 of the last 3 years)	796
NASDAQ	500,000 publicly held shares	$3 million	$750,000 per year	5500
OTC	min. or none	min. or none	min. or none	28,000+

In addition to the NYSE, there are a number of other exchanges in the United States and around the globe. The major exchange in Japan, for example, is known as the Tokyo Exchange. In England there's the London Exchange. Back in the United States, the second biggest exchange based on the total value of traded shares is the American Stock Exchange (AMEX), also based in New York. The AMEX trades 800 different stocks. A third, loosely organized exchange, where newer and smaller stocks are traded, is the OTC, or Over the Counter. Plucked from the more than 28,000 or so OTC stocks are about 5500 more heavily traded companies that switch hands on a nationwide computer-based stock trading network called the National Association of Securities Dealers Automated Quotations system, known as NASDAQ. Even though NASDAQ is home to many young companies, a number of powerful firms like Intel and Microsoft among them, are listed on this exchange.

To be listed on a particular exchange in the United States, a company must meet certain requirements, including the number of individual shareholders or years in which the company has turned a baseline profit. The most stringent guidelines are those of the New York Stock Exchange. It's because of these requirements that this exchange is also referred to glowingly as the "Big Board," a

This will not be on the test. Procter & Gamble, makers of Crest toothpaste, Tide detergent, and Ivory soap, was founded by William Procter and James Gamble back in 1837. They formalized their business operation by putting up $3596.47 apiece. If still around today, the two men might want to cash in on their company's modest growth since its founding. In 1996 the Cincinnati-based manufacturer counted profits of $3.0 billion from $35 billion in worldwide sales.

Source: Procter & Gamble

sign that firms trading there have, in Wall Street-speak, 'made it' financially.

A (Short) History of Stocks

The markets have not always been this complex. The first European stock exchange was established in 1531 in Antwerp, Belgium. In the early 1600s, the Dutch traded shares of the United Dutch East India Company, an organization which was involved in outfitting ships to travel to East India and bring riches back to Europe. Investors–who traded shares on a bridge crossing the Amstel River in Amsterdam–bought shares of the company, hoping that its success would bring them fortunes. In 1773 the first stock exchange in England was founded in London. Until that time, English stock traders conducted their business in coffee-houses.

But in the New World, it was the Dutch who started what would later become the New York

---

The Dow Jones Industrial Average Through the Years

Nothing lasts forever, they say, and that definitely pertains to the companies listed on the DJIA as well. Started over a century ago with just 12 stocks that mirrored the major industries of the day, only one listed back then still remains today: General Electric.

The original 12 companies that comprised the DJIA:

American Cotton Oil	Laclede Gas
American Sugar	National Lead
American Tobacco	North American
Chicago Gas	Tennessee Coal & Iron
Dist. Cattle Feeding	U.S. Leather
General Electric	U.S. Rubber

The current 30:

Allied-Signal	IBM
Alcoa	International Paper
American Express	Johnson & Johnson
AT&T	McDonald's
Boeing	Merck
Caterpillar	Minnesota Mining and
ChevronCoca-Cola	Manufacturing (3M)
Disney, Du Pont	J.P. Morgan
Eastman Kodak	Philip Morris
Exxon	Procter & Gamble
General Electric	Sears
General Motors	Travelers Group
Goodyear	Union Carbide
Hewlett-Packard	United Technologies
	Wal-Mart

Stock Exchange on present-day Manhattan Island. The settlers who traded on the town's northern boundary created a wall in 1653 to protect against attacks from both the Indians and the British. In 1685 a street was laid alongside the wall where trading continued. Later, as the town expanded, the wall was taken down but the name Wall Street remained. It was on May 17, 1792, that organized trading officially commenced when twenty-four stockbrokers signed an agreement to trade with one another and to establish a uniform fee, or commission, rate for their clients. This compact between these traders–which would later grow into the powerful New York Stock Exchange–was allegedly signed beneath a buttonwood tree and is now known as the "Buttonwood Agreement." That's a far cry from today's NYSE, where on a typical day some 500,000,000 shares change hands.

Stock Market Indexes

Tracking the thousands of companies of the various stock exchanges and the millions of shares that trade everyday is an enormous endeavor. But imagine being asked to sum up how the stock market did in the course of one day. Consider having to completely compile all the results quickly and concisely. That was the impetus years ago to create indexes of the exchanges. Like a scientific survey that uses a selected sample to represent a larger, often unmanageable whole, the stock market uses indexes to track the results of the overall market.

These days, when someone asks, "How did the market do today?" they are most likely referring to a famous and widely used index called the Dow Jones Industrial Average (DJIA). An industrialist named

Charles Dow started the index on May 26, 1896, to track 12 stocks that were very important in that day. The index remains today but has grown to 30 stocks, which are determined by the editors of *The Wall Street Journal*, and which are traded on the New York Stock Exchange. The Dow, like other indexes, is designed to measure the performance of a section of the overall stock market. Each index is designed for a different purpose, and many are reported on the evening news and in newspapers that list them. Some of the most popular ones are:

Dow Jones Industrial Average–An average of 30 major stocks traded on the New York Stock Exchange. These 30 stocks represent between 15 and 20 percent of the total value of all stocks traded on the New York Stock Exchange but only about 1 percent of the total number of stocks traded on the exchange. The DJIA is what's called a price weight-averaged index. That means its value is calculated daily by adding the stock prices of all 30 stocks. That figure is then divided by a number that changes to reflect any fluctuations in the number of shares (issuing more shares, stock splits) listed by any of the 30 companies.

Standard & Poor's 500 (S&P 500)–A collection of 500 widely traded stocks. It includes mainly stocks from the New York Stock Exchange, but also some AMEX and OTC/NASDAQ stocks. This value-weighted index represents about 80 percent of the market value of all stocks traded on the New York Stock Exchange. The S&P 500 is more closely followed by many market watchers because they think it more accurately represents the market than the Dow Jones, which only tracks 30 stocks.

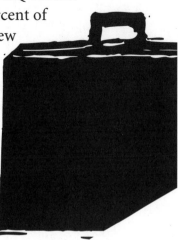

Russell 2000–An index of 2000 smaller U.S. company stocks. This index is used to track how newer companies are doing on the market, compared to the larger firms. Most of these stocks are listed on NASDAQ and OTC.

Wilshire 5000–Measures the performance of all U.S. headquartered equity securities with readily available price data. Over 7000 capitilization-weighted security returns are used to adjust the index making it the most comprehensive of the market measurements.

Doing Your Homework

Investing in any individual stock, like buying a guitar and starting a band, involves a certain level of risk. The degree of risk depends on many factors, not least of which are the characteristics of the company in which you invest. Investing in only one stock is, as your mother might say, akin to putting all your eggs in one basket. Therefore, as should always be the case, you don't want to invest without knowing what that company is all about.

Annual report: *A yearly publication put out by a corporation that provides shareholders with the financial information of a company and a discussion from management about the firm's direction.*

By law, any company that is publicly traded is required to produce certain reports which summarize aspects of its business to the public. One of these is known as an annual report. An annual report tells the story of the company over the last 12 months and chronicles what the organization plans to do in the upcoming year. You can get a copy of an annual report by calling and requesting one from any publicly traded company. A faster way to get financial information about a company is to check out web sites. Most, if not all, publicly traded corporations have World Wide Web home pages, which can be accessed by anyone with a browser and Internet access, usually by typing: *http://www.company name.com.*

<Online Info>

Until recently, most of the helpful information about investing was not available to the individual investor but was the sole province of wealthy clients. Information that was exclusively purchased by brokerage firms for clients was off-limits to most individual investors. With the World Wide Web, there are literally thousands of sites, including the stock exchanges on which the companies are traded, that provide investors with financial information, stock performance, and other valuable market data for a small fee, or often, for free.  Others provide near real-time stock price quotes. Some of the better sites for investors looking to get into stocks include:

General Stock and Company Information

Hoovers On-line *http://www.hoovers.com*

In-house company profiles, earnings reports, and links to over 4000 business web sites.

Cyberstocks *http://www.cyberstocks.com*

Information on Internet-based companies; includes reports, quotes, and profiles.

U.S. Securities and Exchange Commission *http://www.sec.gov*

The government group provides guidelines on investing wisely. Search their database for papers and documents filed by publicly traded companies.

Quote.Com *http://www.quote.com*

Near real-time stock market quotes during trading hours; additional research services, such as Morningstar Mutual Fund Reports, available for a fee.

Stock Market Exchanges

NASDAQ *http://www.nasdaq.com*

Current data of daily trading; loads of company information, including graphs of past price performance.

New York Stock Exchange *http://www.nyse.com*

Links to hundreds of companies listed on the exchange; market stats, glossary.

American Stock Exchange *http://www.amex.com*

Market summaries, company links, even job listings.

</Online Info>

Although they are an excellent starting point for doing research on a particular firm, annual reports (and similar information you find on-line) come with a few caveats. Annual reports are often very attractive, glossy, colorful publications with cool graphics and photos. But be mindful that these publications are produced by the companies themselves (Read: Not-so-subtle advertising here) and need to be viewed critically. It's, therefore, a good idea to turn to other, more objective sources for additional information about a company. One excellent source is a publication called *Value Line Investment Survey* (see box).

Talk of the Street

Like any hobby or trade, the stock market comes complete with a variety of unique concepts and terms. Knowing them is critical to understanding and following a particular stock or the market as a whole. What follows is a starter's list of the terms, many of which appear regularly in the stock tables found in the business section of most newspapers:

The "52-week High-Low"

Usually, the first column in the stock market tables is the 52-week high and low price for a particular stock. These numbers show the range in which the stock price has traded over the previous 52-week, or one-year, period. For example, the fictitious IntraWeb stock may list 60 3/4 and 42 1/8 as its 52-week high and low prices. The first number is the year high, the second is the year low. During the year the stock fluctuated a total of about $18.

**The Stock Bible:
Value Line Investment Survey.**

Between financial journals, television, the Internet, even friends and colleagues, there's no dearth of stock analysis and "tips." Trouble is that much of this material is difficult for the beginner investor to understand or too clouded in opinion. That's one reason why for stock research *Value Line Investment Survey* stands above the rest—and is so popular. This weekly publication compiles and reports information on industries as well as individual stocks in an easy-to-read, one-page-per-company layout (see sample on following page). This relevant data includes assessments of a company's current and future financial status, past stock prices and dividends, and stock price performance over the past decade (if the stock has been around that long). *Value Line* also gives each company a rating that estimates a stock's expected performance for the next year. *Value Line* is not cheap, however (it costs about $570 a year to subscribe). But you can also find it at most libraries in the finance or reference section. For more information on the *Value Line* publication, or to get a trial subscription, call (800) 634-3583.

CLOROX CO. NYSE-CLX | **RECENT PRICE** 75 | **P/E RATIO** 28.4 (Trailing: 31.1 / Median: 15.0) | **RELATIVE P/E RATIO** 1.54 | **DIV'D YLD** 1.7% | **VALUE LINE** 958 | 110

US SERVICE

10/9
15:15

TIMELINESS 3 Average (Relative Price Perform-ance Next 12 Mos.)	High:	15.1	18.0	16.9	22.3	22.7	21.2	26.0	27.7	29.8	39.6	55.1	75.4		Target Price Range 2000 2001 2002
	Low:	11.0	11.8	13.1	15.1	16.1	17.5	19.8	22.0	23.5	27.6	35.0	48.6		

SAFETY 1 Highest (Scale: 1 Highest to 5 Lowest)
BETA .95 (1.00 = Market)

2000-02 PROJECTIONS

	Price	Gain	Ann'l Total Return
High	75	(Nil)	2%
Low	60	(-20%)	-3%

Insider Decisions

	N	D	J	F	M	A	M	J	J
to Buy	0	0	0	1	0	0	0	0	0
Options	3	0	13	5	0	0	3	1	0
to Sell	2	1	12	6	0	0	3	2	0

Institutional Decisions

	4Q'96	1Q'97	2Q'97
to Buy	123	115	128
to Sell	125	137	130
Hld's(000)	48777	49828	48411

Percent shares traded: 9.0 / 6.0 / 3.0

12.0 x "Cash Flow" p sh
2-for-1 split
Relative Price Strength
Shaded area indicates recession

Options: PHLE

© VALUE LINE PUB., INC.

1981	1982	1983	1984	1985	1986	1987	1988	1989	1990	1991	1992	1993	1994	1995	1996	1997	1998		00-02
7.78	9.06	9.45	9.27	9.97	10.21	10.51	11.66	12.24	13.73	15.19	15.74	14.90	17.21	18.59	21.63	22.85	25.70	Sales per sh A	33.80
.56	.75	.88	.94	1.05	1.15	1.27	1.57	1.72	1.88	2.01	2.14	2.29	2.57	2.85	3.30	3.39	4.00	"Cash Flow" per sh	5.45
.42	.49	.68	.75	.82	.90	.98	1.23	1.32	1.40	1.22	1.33	1.54	1.68	1.89	2.14	2.41	2.75	Earnings per sh B	3.90
.20	.22	.24	.27	.31	.35	.40	.46	.55	.65	.74	.80	.86	.93	.96	1.06	1.16	1.28	Div'ds Decl'd per sh C ■	1.75
.36	.39	.31	.35	.39	.61	.52	.85	.79	1.44	1.01	1.14	.71	.53	.59	.83	.86	.90	Cap'l Spending per sh	1.15
2.73	2.94	3.37	4.10	4.59	5.15	5.76	6.60	7.10	7.50	7.24	7.46	8.02	8.52	8.84	9.10	9.35	10.80	Book Value per sh D	16.50
91.81	95.75	96.71	105.19	105.80	106.69	107.11	108.09	110.80	108.06	108.39	109.09	109.70	106.74	106.74	102.52	110.84	111.00	Common Shs Outst'g E	111.00
6.7	6.1	8.8	9.3	9.3	13.0	14.2	12.0	12.4	14.6	15.7	16.1	15.1	15.6	14.9	17.9	22.4		Avg Ann'l P/E Ratio	17.0
.81	.67	.74	.87	.76	.88	.95	1.00	.94	1.08	1.00	.98	.89	1.02	1.00	1.12	1.31		Relative P/E Ratio	1.20
7.3%	7.2%	4.0%	3.9%	4.1%	3.0%	2.8%	3.1%	3.4%	3.1%	3.9%	3.7%	3.7%	3.6%	3.4%	2.8%	2.1%		Avg Ann'l Div'd Yield	2.6%

CAPITAL STRUCTURE as of 6/30/97

Total Debt $939.4 mill. Due in 5 Yrs $923.9 mill.
LT Debt $565.9 mill. LT Interest $50.0 mill.
(LT interest earned: 9.3x; total interest coverage: 8.5x)
(35% of Cap'l)

Leases, Uncapitalized Annual rentals $9.9 mill.
Pension Liability None

Pfd Stock None

Common Stock 110,844,589 shs. (65% of Cap'l)
(adjusted for 9/97 2-for-1 split)

						1126.0	1259.9	1356.3	1484.0	1646.5	1717.0	1634.2	1836.9	1984.2	2217.8	2532.7	2850	Sales ($mill) A	3750
						18.2%	19.4%	18.5%	18.0%	19.7%	20.1%	23.3%	22.9%	23.3%	24.0%	23.4%	25.5%	Operating Margin	26.0%
						31.4	37.5	44.7	50.1	87.0	89.6	83.6	94.1	103.9	116.5	126.4	135	Depreciation ($mill)	175
						104.9	132.6	145.6	153.6	131.3	143.8	167.9	180.0	200.8	222.1	249.4	305	Net Profit ($mill)	435
						43.8%	37.4%	36.6%	36.9%	37.9%	40.4%	39.0%	41.3%	40.6%	40.0%	40.0%	40.0%	Income Tax Rate	40.0%
						9.3%	10.5%	10.7%	10.4%	8.0%	8.4%	10.3%	9.8%	10.1%	10.0%	9.8%	9.8%	Net Profit Margin	11.6%
						257.2	189.9	284.0	192.8	118.4	d3.2	160.2	128.5	121.0	d50.0	d219.2	d100	Working Cap'l ($mill)	d100
						26.6	29.2	7.1	7.5	406.8	262.3	254.7	216.1	253.1	356.3	565.9	900	Long-Term Debt ($mill)	900
						616.5	712.9	786.2	810.5	784.3	813.7	879.3	909.4	943.9	932.8	1036.0	1200	Net Worth ($mill)	1830
						16.6%	18.0%	18.5%	18.8%	12.2%	14.3%	15.5%	16.7%	17.7%	18.5%	17.1%	16.0%	% Earned Total Cap'l	17.0%
						17.0%	18.6%	18.5%	19.0%	16.7%	17.7%	19.1%	19.8%	21.3%	23.8%	24.1%	25.5%	% Earned Net Worth	24.0%
						10.2%	11.6%	10.9%	10.2%	6.6%	7.1%	8.5%	9.1%	10.4%	12.0%	12.5%	13.5%	% Retained to Com Eq	13.0%
						40%	37%	41%	46%	61%	60%	56%	54%	51%	50%	48%	47%	% All Div'ds to Net Prof	45%

CURRENT POSITION (SMILL.)

	1995	1996	6/30/97
Cash Assets	137.3	90.8	101.0
Receivables	311.9	315.2	357.1
Inventory (LIFO)	121.1	138.8	170.3
Other	30.0	29.1	45.1
Current Assets	600.3	573.9	673.5
Accts Payable	122.8	155.4	143.4
Debt Due	115.7	193.0	373.5
Other	240.8	275.5	375.8
Current Liab.	479.3	623.9	892.7

ANNUAL RATES

of change (per sh)	Past 10 Yrs.	Past 5 Yrs.	Est'd '95-'97 to '00-'02
Sales	7.5%	7.0%	10.0%
"Cash Flow"	10.5%	9.5%	11.5%
Earnings	9.0%	8.0%	13.0%
Dividends	11.5%	8.0%	10.5%
Book Value	6.0%	4.0%	12.5%

QUARTERLY SALES ($ mill.) A

Fiscal Year Ends	Sep.30	Dec.31	Mar.31	Jun.30	Full Fiscal Year
1994	449.7	370.9	481.9	534.4	1836.9
1995	476.4	414.5	499.1	594.2	1984.2
1996	518.5	466.8	560.1	672.4	2217.8
1997	590.8	530.2	649.2	762.5	2532.7
1998	675	600	725	850	2850

EARNINGS PER SHARE A B

Fiscal Year Ends	Sep.30	Dec.31	Mar.31	Jun.30	Full Fiscal Year
1994	.43	.29	.47	.49	1.68
1995	.50	.32	.51	.56	1.89
1996	.56	.37	.58	.63	2.14
1997	.63	.42	.64	.72	2.41
1998	.70	.50	.72	.83	2.75

QUARTERLY DIVIDENDS PAID C ■

Cal-endar	Mar.31	Jun.30	Sep.30	Dec.31	Full Year
1993	.21	.225	.225	.225	.89
1994	.225	.225	.24	.24	.93
1995	.24	.24	.265	.265	1.01
1996	.265	.265	.29	.29	1.11
1997	.29	.29	.32		

BUSINESS: The Clorox Co. is a major producer of household goods. Prods. incl. Clorox 2 bleach, Liquid-plumr, Formula 409, Clorox Pre-Wash, Soft Scrub, Tilex, Pine-Sol, Combat, Black Flag insecticides, Kingsford and Match Light charcoal, K.C. Masterpiece barbecue sauce, Hidden Valley Ranch salad dressing, Fresh Step cat litter, Brita water filtration systems, Armor All auto appearance products. Largest segments: home cleaning & auto appearance, 27% '97 sales; laundry, 21%. Adv., 13.8% of sales. '97 depr. rate: 12.1%. Est'd plant age: 4 years. Has about 5,500 employees, 13,350 shareholders. HC Investments controls 29.9% of common shares (9/97 proxy). Chmn. & C.E.O.: G. Craig Sullivan. Inc.: CA. Addr.: 1221 Broadway, Oakland, CA 94612. Tel.: 510-271-7000.

Clorox shares have been hot, even relative to the generally strong blue-chip sector of the stock market. Interestingly, although Clorox has increased its efforts in overseas markets (to 16% of sales at present, up from 4% in '92) and would like to progress further (to at least 20% by 2000) with emphasis on Latin America and Asia, its percentage (which is small compared to some other giant consumer products companies) shields CLX shares from the choppiness some others have experienced recently in response to uncertainties regarding currency translations. Besides serving as a sort-of refuge from currency worries, the main attraction here has been Wall Street's realization that the vision announced by Craig Sullivan when he became C.E.O. in mid-1992 is actually translating to accelerating earnings growth. Looking ahead, we still like the earnings story, as most businesses continue to report healthy profit trends. But valuation issues have become increasingly problematic for the neutrally ranked stock. **The company is doing a great job in deciding on which businesses it should focus.** This was a big issue when Mr. Sullivan took the helm, as he openly criticized what had previously been a lack of focus. But the company now understands that its rivals are big and powerful, and that it needs to pick its spots. Focusing on such areas as household cleansers, insecticides, and laundry bleach, the company now derives 85% of its business from markets where its brands rank number one or two. And there are good things even about some of the other businesses. CLX isn't in the top two in the overall cat litter market, but it is one or two in some sectors, and the business is a generally healthy one. CLX's Hidden Valley label is running neck-and-neck for third position in salad dressing, but it is huge in one subsegment; ranch dressings. **The company has shown itself to be a skilled acquirer.** Past purchases of Black Flag and Combat give it a strong position in insecticides. The Brita purchase gave CLX the top brand in the emerging market for low-cost home water filters. And the most recent purchase, Armor All, gives CLX access to a whole new distribution channel, auto supplies retailers.
Marc H. Gerstein   October 17, 1997

(A) Fiscal year ends June 30. (B) Based on average shares outstanding. Next earnings report due late Oct. Excl. nonrecurring gain (loss): '82, ($0.02); '83, $0.01; '84, $0.03; '91, ($0.73); '92, $0.42. (C) Next dividend meeting about Jan. 15. Goes ex about Jan. 25. Dividend payment dates: Feb. 15, May 15, Aug. 15, Nov. 15. ■ Div'd reinvest. plan available. (D) Incl. intangibles. In '97: $1187.0 mill., $10.70/sh. (E) In mill., adj. for stock splits.

Company's Financial Strength	A+
Stock's Price Stability	90
Price Growth Persistence	100
Earnings Predictability	95

Source: Value Line Investment survey. Reprinted by permission.

These stock prices give you some insight into how much the price of a stock has moved in the past year. A stock which over the previous 52 weeks has traded between 51 and 61 might be a lot less volatile than a stock which has traded between, say, 6 and 56 over the same period. Some investors also look to see where a stock is currently trading compared to its year high and low, opting not to buy if it's near the high end for fear that it might fall.

Unlike the rest of the United States business world, which buys and sells goods at full-cent prices, stocks historically have been traded in 1/8 dollar increments: 1/8, 1/4, 3/8, 1/2, 5/8, 3/4, 7/8, and 1. Some shares that are traded at very low prices, like many listed on NASDAQ, for example, may actually drop to increments of 1/16 or 1/32. Regardless of the fraction used, all of these prices refer to the dollar equivalents: 1/8 equals 12.5 cents; 5/8 equals 62.5 cents; 3/4 equals 75 cents, and so forth. For instance, shares of Sears might end the day dropping 3/4 ($.75) to 45 1/2 ($45.50); IBM stock's price

Good-bye Fractions.
Hello Decimals.

The New York Stock Exchange announced on June 5, 1997, that it would abandon its 200-year-old tradition of pricing stocks with fractions such as "¼" or "½" and begin using the decimal equivalents like ".25" and ".50," respectively. IBM stock, for example, which might be currently listed at 130 ½ will soon be listed the way that everything else in the country is priced, in decimals. In this case, at 130.50. The NYSE move to decimals will occur no later than the year 2000, and could even happen sooner if the exchange feels that they are technically ready to make the move. For the ordinary investor, the long term effects will not be known for some time, but the system will certainly be easier for consumers to understand (How often do you buy a 7-11 Big Gulp in fractional pricing?), and could even mean some savings. That's because specialists, those who execute a majority of the trades conducted on the floor of the exchange, are currently limited to handling trades in increments of 6 ¼ cents per share. The margin between the highest price that a trader will buy a stock–the bid–and the lowest price at which one is willing to sell–the asking price–is the traders profit for each share that they sell. Smaller increments of pricing, a benefit of decimal pricing, would allow a smaller spread which could result in savings. Most likely, the increments will be measured in nickels so that trades could be executed at prices such as 15.10, 15.05 and 15.15. Several studies have shown that investors could save between $1.5 to $4 billion a year as a result of this fraction-to-decimal pricing change. Think this is an innovative idea? The United States is the only major country that does not yet trade stocks in decimals. Who knows, the metric system may not be far behind.

might end the day gaining 2 7/8 ($2.875) to 100 7/8 ($100.875). Incidentally, the use of 1/8 increments dates back to the late 1700s when the Spanish-milled dollar was the popular currency of the time. The gold coin was literally cut into halves, quarters, and eighths with a hammer and chisel for the purpose of trading it. Only the stock market uses this somewhat confusing counting method today.

The smallest fraction used for pricing stocks on the major exchanges and makets was 1/8. Some very small stocks were traded on increments dipping down to 1/16 or even 1/32. However, in 1997, the American Stock Exchange, NASDAQ and The New York Stock Exchange announced that they will begin using the 1/16 fraction as well. One reason for this move deals with something called the "spread" which is the price between what buyers bidding price and the sellers asking price on a given stock. But more importantly than this jump in fraction pricing was the NYSE's announcement to drop fractional pricing altogether in favor of decimal pricing (see box).

PROFILE
• • • • • • • • • •

Chris Nicita, 31
San Francisco, California

Starting your own company can be risky, but the rewards can be sweet. In 1996 Chris Nicita quit his health-care consulting job on the east coast to launch a new bio-tech consulting firm called BioMedical Insights, Inc., in California. For start-up seed money, Chris cashed out all of his $12,000 from his existing 401(k) plan, losing about 30 percent to taxes and penalties. For five months, when cash was tight, neither he nor his fellow employees received a paycheck. Later, as money started coming in, Chris started investing some of his growing income. The Detroit native opened an account through Charles Schwab discount brokers. Through this account, Chris invests into both mutual funds (he's currently in four funds, including a Janus (800-525-3713) overseas fund and Fidelity (800-544-8888) electronics sector fund) and stocks. Chris acknowledges the risk of stocks but feels equally qualified investing in companies in the bio-tech industry, which he understands and follows closely. As for making trades, Chris usually does it online, which he says is easy, fun, and cheaper than the phone-based alternative. As of early 1997, Chris had $10,000 in four mutual funds, $5000 in three stocks, $5000 in a liquid money market account, and a business to call his own.

Stock Symbol

Rather than using the full name of each company, which in some cases would be prohibitively long, each company traded on one of the stock exchanges is given a truncated letter grouping known as a ticker symbol. A few examples are: F = Ford, RBK = Reebok, and TOY = Toys-R-Us. There are exceptions, but in general, stocks traded on the New York Stock Exchange are represented by one- to three-letter symbols, and those on the NASDAQ by four- or five-letter symbols. In general, older, more established companies will be traded on the New York Stock Exchange, while smaller companies will be traded on NASDAQ or the American Stock Exchange.

P/E Ratio

As noted earlier, one of the ways in which a company rewards its shareholders is by giving them a slice of the profits, or earnings, through dividends.

What's in a Name?

Aside from the more formal classifications of stock, such as "common stock" and "preferred stock," which pertain to fundamental differences between the two types of shares, there are also a number of labels to describe different kinds of stocks and their various characteristics. Some of these more frequently used monikers include:

Blue chip stock: Taken directly from the blue chip in poker, the most valuable one, these stocks have a long history of profits and dividends. Usually older, more established companies like IBM or General Electric are known as Blue Chips.

Growth stock: As the name implies, these stocks are expected to achieve better-than- average capital appreciation, or share price increases, due to higher profits and expansion than other companies. They are also riskier investments than Blue Chip stocks.

Income stock: Usually pertaining to utility firms, like telephone or electric companies with very consistent cash flows, these stocks have a history of paying high dividends, also known as income.

Penny stock: Although they may not literally trade for pennies a share, new stocks with little history that also have the potential for huge returns or losses for their investors are referred to as penny stocks.

Cyclical and noncyclical stock: When the economy sours, a manufacturer that produces expensive durable goods such as automobiles may see sales drop, while firms that produce staple products like food aren't bothered as much (a penny-pinching household will focus income on food, not new cars, when times are tough). Those companies like the automobile makers are said to be cyclical, because the company performance is tethered to the cycles of the economy. On the other hand, a firm whose stock price weathers the up and downs is known as noncyclical.

When a company announces quarterly earnings, it can report them two different ways: total earnings or earnings per share. Earnings per share represent the total earnings that a company produced divided by the number of shares outstanding. For instance, suppose our imaginary software company called IntraWeb announced quarterly earnings, or profit, of $2 million dollars. If the firm had exactly one million shares of stock outstanding, the earnings per share would be $2 ($2 million ÷ 1 million shares = $2). The price-earnings ratio is simply this figure, as compared to the actual price at which the stock is currently trading. So if IntraWeb stock is trading at $30 a share, the P/E ratio, or price earnings ratio, would be 15: Price ($30) ÷ Earnings ($2) = 15. The P/E ratio of a stock can give insight into how much a stock is trading above its actual earnings. The higher the P/E, the more investors are paying on speculation of future income and less on present earnings. Young companies, incidentally, may have very high P/E's, indicating that investors are banking on future prospects, not current income. Historically, the average stock market P/E ratio, is about 14. Companies that have not declared a profit do not have P/E ratios and the line may be left blank or have a "..." in the newspaper column.

NEW YORK STOCK EXCHANGE COMPOSITE TRANSACTIONS

	52 Weeks Hi	Lo	Stock	Sym	Div	Yld %	PE	Vol 100s	Hi	Lo	Close	Net Chg
n	26⅝	24⅝	SJG CapTr pf			...	...	36	26	25¾	25⅞	...
	74¾	58⅜	SPS Tech	ST		...	19	59	74⅝	74	74½	+ ½
	25	13½	SPS TransSvc	PAY		...	27	157	19⅜	19	19¼	...
	70⅝	21⅜	SPX Cp	SPW	j	...	dd	870	67¾	66½	67½	− ⅜
n	25¼	24⅝	SWEPCO pfA			...	...	415	25	25	25	− ⅛
	14	9⅛	SabineRTr	SBR	1.67e	12.4	11	241	13⅞	13½	13½	− ½
n	33⅜	23¼	SabreGp A	TSG		...	...	1313	27¾	27⅛	27¼	...
s	45⅛	16⅞	♣SafegrdSci	SFE		...	54	796	29⅝	28¾	29½	+ ¾
	18⅝	14⅛	SafetyKln	SK	.36	2.2	16	920	16⅛	16	16⅛	...
	52	31⅝	Safeway	SWY		...	23	5661	48⅝	47¼	47⅜	− 1⅜
	20¾	14⅝	SagaPete A	SPMA	.47e	2.5	...	92	19⅜	18⅞	18⅞	− ½
	18⅞	13½	SagaPete B	SPMB	.47e	2.8	...	29	17¼	17	17	− ⅜
s	84⅝	52¾	StJoe	SJP	.20	.2	22	115	83½	82⅛	82⅜	− 1⅜
	51¾	35⅞	StJohnKnits	SJK	.10	.2	27	545	48¾	48⅛	48⅜	+ ⅛
	43¼	28¾	StJudeMed	STJ	j	...	38	4635	38	36⅝	37¾	+ 1
	80¼	50⅝	StPaulCos	SPC	1.88	2.4	15	1226	79¾	78⅝	78⅞	− 1¼
	71	51	StPaul MIPS		3.00	4.3	...	570	70½	70	70	− ⅝
s	17¼	13⅞	StJoeL&P	SAJ	.96	5.8	13	8	16⅝	16⅜	16⅝	+ ⅛
	41¼	18⅝	SaksHldgs	SKS		...	28	5603	23	22⅛	22⅛	− ¾
	5⅜	2¾	♣Salant	SLT		...	dd	38	3	2⅞	3	...
	137¾	69¼	SallieM	SLM	1.76	1.3	17	4032	134⅜	133½	134¼	+ ⅛
	44	36¾	SallieM pf		2.50	6.1	...	2	41¼	41¼	41¼	+ ⅜
	9⅞	8⅜	SalomonWld	SBG	.88a	9.0	...	963	9⅞	9⅝	9¾	...
	17¼	13⅛	SalomonSBF	SBF	3.80e	22.4	...	565	17⅛	17	17	...
	16½	14⅝	SalomonHIF	HIF	1.50a	9.2	...	130	16¼	16⅛	16¼	...
	15¾	12¾	SalomnWldInc	SBW	1.43a	9.2	...	456	15⅝	15½	15½	...
	61⅜	38	SalomonInc	SB	.64	1.1	6	2255	57½	56½	56⅝	− ⅞
	26¼	23⅝	Salomon dep pfD		2.02	8.0	...	39	25½	25⅜	25⅜	...
	27½	23¾	Salomon dep pfE		2.10	7.9	...	65	26⅞	26⅝	26⅝	...
n	27¼	24½	Salomon pfG		2.38	9.0	...	84	26⅜	26¼	26⅜	+ ⅛
n	65½	53¾	Salomon DECS	CXB	3.48	5.7	...	4	61¾	61¼	61¼	− ¼
	8⅞	5⅞	SanJuanBsn	SJT	1.18e	14.7	...	324	8	7⅞	8	...
	30½	12⅜	♣SaAnitRlty	SAR	.80	2.7	dd	285	29⅞	29¾	29¾	− ¼
	16	10½	♣SntaFeEngy	SFR		...	cc	5930	15⅛	14⅞	15⅛	+ ⅛
	20½	17⅛	SntaFe SPERS	SFF	1.96e	9.7	...	97	20⅛	19⅞	20⅛	+ ⅛
n	33¼	31	SantaFeInt	SDC		...	...	16939	32⅛	31⅛	31¾	+ ⅝
	39¼	34	♣SaFePacPipe	SFL	3.00	7.9	16	55	38⅜	38	38⅛	...
	31	21⅞	SantaIsabel	ISA	.34e	1.1	...	183	29⅝	29½	29⅝	...
n	25¾	25¼	SantndrFnl prfG		.29p	...	...	231	25½	25¼	25¼	− ⅛
n	26⅝	24¼	SantdrFin pfF		2.03	8.1	...	485	25⅜	25⅛	25⅛	− ⅛
	24¼	21⅛	SantdrFin prA		1.84	8.0	...	43	23⅜	23⅛	23⅛	− ⅛
	25⅝	22⅜	SantdrFin prB		1.98	8.0	...	79	25	24⅝	24⅝	− ⅛
	26⅛	23⅛	SantdrFin prC		2.03	8.0	...	2752	25⅝	25⅛	25⅜	...
n	27⅞	24¼	SantdrFin prD		2.19	8.1	...	1825	26⅞	26⅝	26⅞	− ⅛
n	27¼	24⅜	SantdrFin prE		2.14	8.1	...	51	26½	26⅜	26⅜	− ⅛
	26⅝	24¾	Santandr pfB		2.18	8.5	...	12	25¾	25¾	25¾	...
	27¼	25½	Santandr pfC		2.24	8.4	...	20	26¾	26⅝	26⅝	+ ⅛
	26¼	23⅞	Santandr pfD		2.00	7.8	...	6	25⅜	25⅜	25⅜	...
	43⅜	30	SaraLee	SLE	.84	2.0	21	10095	42½	42	42	− ½
	17⅝	12⅝	SaulCenters	BFS	1.56	9.2	30	261	17	16⅝	17	+ ¼
▲	16¾	11¼	SavanFood	SFI	.15f	.9	37	833	17⅜	16⅝	17¼	+ ⅝
	29¾	22⅞	Sbarro	SBA	1.08	3.7	16	121	29½	29¼	29⅜	...
	28¼	23⅜	SCANA	SCG	1.51	6.1	13	996	25	24⅝	24⅞	− ⅛
	30	23½	Scania A	SCVA	.71e	2.4	...	32	29⅛	29	29	− ⅞
	30¼	23¼	Scania B	SCVB	.71e	2.4	...	27	29¼	29	29	− ⅞
	9⅛	6⅝	Schawk A	SGK	.26	3.0	dd	23	8⅞	8¾	8¾	− ¼
	62	39½	Scherer	SHR		...	23	776	54⅝	54⅛	54⅜	− ⅜
s▲	48¾	26⅞	ScheringPl	SGP	.76	1.6	28	11949	48⅞	47¼	48⅜	− ⅛
	126¼	79⅜	♣Schlumbgr	SLB	1.50	1.2	32	9215	123⅞	121⅛	123⅛	+ 1⅛
n	63	60	Schlumbgr wi			...	...	1	61½	61½	61½	...
	13⅛	11¼	SchroderAsian	SHF	.09p	...	...	898	12½	12⅜	12⅜	...
	42⅝	19⅞	SchwabC	SCH	.20	.5	30	3107	42¼	41¼	41⅞	− ½
	39½	27⅜	ShwtzMaud	SWM	.60	1.5	15	728	39⅛	38⅞	38⅞	− ⅛
	33¾	15¾	SciGameHldg	SG		...	12	468	21	20¾	20⅞	− ⅛
▲	22	12	♣SciAtlanta	SFA	.06	.3	62	12777	23	21⅝	23	+ 1⅛
n	43½	34	Scor Adr	SCO	1.74e	4.4	...	42	40¼	39¾	39⅞	− ⅞
	29⅜	19½	♣Scotsman	SCT	.10	.4	15	370	27⅜	27⅛	27¼	− ¼
	2⅞	1⅛	♣ScotLiqdGld	SGD		...	50	10	2½	2½	2½	+ ⅛
	30	16¾	ScottsCo	SMG		...	...	685	28	27⅞	28	...

	52 Weeks Hi	Lo	Stock	Sym	Div	Yld %	PE	Vol 100s	Hi	Lo	Close	Net Chg
n	19⅞	15¼	Steinway	LVB		...	17	257	18⅞	18⅝	18¾	...
▲	21⅞	16⅞	Stepan	SCL	.50	2.3	13	28	22	21⅝	22	+ ¼
	19⅛	10¼	SterlBcp	STL	.36	2.1	15	72	17½	17½	17½	− ¼
	40	24⅛	SterlingCmrc	SE		...	38	4812	33⅜	32⅝	33	+ ⅝
	14½	10 5/16	SterlElec	SEC	stk	...	9	93	12½	12⅛	12⅛	...
s	34⅝	20⅞	SterlSftwr	SSW		...	13	3394	32⅛	31⅜	32	+ ⅛
	54⅞	30¼	StetSocieta	STE	.77e	1.4	...	169	54¾	53⅞	54⅜	...
	40½	23½	StetSocieta A	STEA	.89e	2.6	...	10	34	34	34	− 1¼
	22⅝	18¾	♣StewInfo	STC	.24	1.2	11	30	20½	20½	20½	...
	9	6⅛	Stifel Fnl	SF	.12b	1.5	7	18	8⅛	8	8⅛	...
▲	14¼	13	StoklyVC pr		1.00	6.9	...	4	14½	14½	14½	+ ¼
	45⅜	28⅝	♣StoneWeb	SW	.60	1.3	dd	173	45	44½	44⅞	+ ⅛
	17¼	9½	StoneCont	STO	.45j	...	dd	4624	14½	14	14	− ⅝
	20⅝	12¼	StoneCont pfE		1.31j	...	...	64	17⅜	17⅛	17⅛	− ¼
	30	17¾	StoneEngy	SGY		...	33	117	28⅜	28¼	28⅜	...
	54⅜	**30**	**StorTch**	**STK**		...	**14**	**6880**	**43½**	**40⅞**	**43½**	**+ 2¾**
	27⅞	19⅞	♣StorageTr	SEA	1.74	6.7	...	310	26⅛	25⅝	26⅛	+ ⅜
	40⅜	32	StorageUSA	SUS	2.40	6.0	19	663	40⅜	39¾	40	+ ⅛
	12⅝	11⅛	StrtGlob	SGL	1.14	9.1	...	332	12⅝	12½	12½	...
	49⅝	16⅝	♣StratusCptr	SRA		...	24	2188	48⅛	46¾	48	+ 1¼
	15⅞	6⅝	StrideRite	SRR	.20	1.5	cc	5330	13⅝	13⅜	13½	− ⅛
	44	32	StudLoan	STU	.48	1.1	13	104	43½	42¾	42¾	− ¼
s	26⅞	14¾	♣SturmRgr	RGR	.80	4.4	16	1005	18⅜	17⅞	18	− ¼
	21⅞	17	SuburbnPrpn	SPH	2.00	11.3	26	1036	18⅜	17¾	17¾	− ⅝
	36¾	15¾	♣SuizaFood	SZA		...	10	312	34⅞	34¼	34¼	− ⅝
	52¼	32⅝	SummitBcp	SUB	1.44	2.8	16	1852	51⅞	51⅜	51¾	...
	22½	18	♣SummitProp	SMT	1.59	8.1	20	1031	19⅞	19⅝	19¾	...
	31⅝	21⅞	SunCo	SUN	1.00	3.2	dd	2982	31⅝	31¼	31⅜	− ¼
	30½	23¼	SunCo pfA		1.80	6.0	...	1355	30½	30	30¼	...
	5⅛	1⅞	SunCoastInd	SN		...	dd	8	4⅛	4	4	...
	34¾	25⅝	♣SunCmnty	SUI	1.88	5.4	26	291	34⅝	34½	34⅝	...
	5⅝	3⅞	SunEngy	SLP	.30e	5.9	11	330	5¼	5⅛	5⅛	...
	17⅝	11½	SunHlthcr	SHG		...	38	2262	17½	17	17⅜	...
	54¼	29⅛	SunIntHtl	SIH		...	21	389	37⅝	36¾	37⅛	− ⅜
s	51	26⅛	SunAmerica	SAI	.40	.8	23	4138	50¾	49½	50	− ⅜
	109¼	70	SunAmerica pfE		3.10	2.9	...	24	108½	108	108¼	+ ¼
	26¼	24¼	SunAm TOPrS V		2.09	8.1	...	49	25⅞	25⅝	25¾	+ ⅛
n	26	24½	SunAm TOPrS W		2.08	8.1	...	276	26	25¾	25¾	− ⅛
n	44⅜	37½	SunAm PERCS	SIP	1.53p	...	...	454	44	43¼	43¾	...
	39	12	Sunbeam	SOC	.04	.1	dd	8428	37⅞	37⅛	37⅞	+ ¼
s	26¾	15	♣Suncor g	SU	.68	...	...	42	26¼	25¾	26¼	+ ¼
	59¼	32½	Sundstrand	SNS	.68	1.2	29	2188	58¾	58⅜	58½	− ⅛
	50¾	35⅜	♣SunGard	SDS		...	50	1428	44⅞	44⅜	44¾	− ⅛
	19⅞	9½	SunriseMed	SMD		...	dd	111	14	13¾	14	+ ¼
	1½	¾	SunshMin	SSC		...	11	647	⅞	13/16	⅞	...
	12	10¼	Sunsource A	SDP	1.10	9.5	...	112	11⅝	11½	11⅝	...
	5¼	4	Sunsource B	SDPB	.36	7.4	15	245	5	4⅞	4⅞	− ⅛
	14⅛	9½	♣SunstnHtlInv	SSI	1.00	7.3	19	1015	13¾	13½	13⅝	− ⅛
	57⅝	34⅞	SunTrustBk	STI	.90	1.6	20	2041	57⅝	56⅞	57	− ½
	27⅞	21⅝	SupInd	SUP	.28f	1.0	15	472	26⅞	26½	26⅞	...
n	28¼	16	SuperTele	SUT		...	...	131	27	26¾	27	...
n	19⅛	17¾	SprmrcdsUni	UNR		...	...	28	18⅝	18½	18½	− ¼
	36⅝	27⅛	♣Supervalu	SVU	1.00	2.8	14	1472	35½	35⅛	35¼	− ⅜
	24¾	22	SvenskExp pf		1.84	7.8	...	189	23⅝	23¼	23½	+ ⅛
	37⅝	17¼	SwiftEngy	SFY	p	...	17	170	26⅝	26⅜	26⅝	...
n	19½	13¼	♣SwisherIntGp	SWR		...	...	159	19⅜	18⅞	18⅞	− ⅝
	24½	19½	♣SwissHelvFd	SWZ	1.02e	4.2	...	598	24⅜	24¼	24¼	− ⅛
▲	37	23⅛	♣SybronInt	SYB		...	25	1956	38	36⅝	37⅝	+ ⅞
s	**36⅞**	**25¼**	**SymbolTech**	**SBL**	**.03p**	...	**26**	**769**	**33¾**	**31¾**	**33⅝**	**+ 1⅝**
	10¼	6¾	SymsCp	SYM		...	9	10	9½	9½	9½	+ ⅛
s▲	28¼	14⅜	SynovusFnl	SNV	.36	1.3	24	633	28⅜	27¾	28⅜	+ ⅛
	38¼	27⅝	SyscoCp	SYY	.60	1.6	23	2332	37¾	37⅛	37¼	− ¾
			-T-T-T-									
	16½	7⅜	TB Woods	TBW	.32	2.3	11	138	14¼	13⅞	14	− ¼
	6½	3¾	TCBY Ent	TBY	.20	3.3	19	359	6¼	6⅛	6⅛	− ⅛
	2½	1½	TCC Ind	TEL		...	dd	25	2⅜	2⅜	2⅜	...
▲	47¾	31⅛	♣TCF Fnl	TCB	1.00f	2.1	19	1164	47⅞	47	47⅝	− ⅛
	25⅛	19¾	TCI Comm TOPrS		2.18	8.8	...	742	24⅞	24⅝	24¾	...

	52 Weeks Hi	Lo	Stock	Sym	Div	Yld %	PE	Vol 100s	Hi	Lo	Close	Net Chg
n	27	24½	TrnsCan TOPrS		2.19	8.2	...	38	26¾	26⅝	26¾	+ ¼
	20⅜	14½	♣TransCda g	TRP	1.16	...	...	281	20⅛	20	20⅛	...
n▲	26⅜	24¼	TransCda COPrS		2.13	8.2	...	60	26½	26⅛	26⅛	− ⅛
▲	15	9¾	TrancntlRlty	TCI	.28	1.8	dd	63	15½	14¾	15⅜	+ ½
	16	7⅝	♣TransitlHosp	THY		...	dd	106	16	15⅞	15⅞	...
	8¾	3¼	Transmedia	TMN	.04	.9	55	84	4½	4¼	4⅜	+ ⅛
	74⅝	46¾	♣Transocean	RIG	.24	.3	30	5032	73½	70⅝	72¾	+ 1⅜
	8⅝	4⅝	TrnspMritma	TMM	.18e	3.1	6	935	5⅞	5¾	5⅞	+ ⅛
	7¼	3⅞	TrnspMritma A	TMMA	.18e	3.7	...	275	4⅞	4¾	4⅞	+ ⅛
	14	11	TrnspGas	TGS	.98e	8.1	...	152	12¼	12	12⅛	− ⅛
	10	5½	TransPro	TPR	.20	2.4	7	56	8¼	8⅛	8¼	+ ¼
	22⅞	17	TransTech	TT	.26	1.2	12	80	21	20⅝	20⅞	+ ⅛
s	64¼	29 1/16	Travelers	TRV	.60	.9	17	17700	63⅞	61⅝	63⅜	+ 1⅛
	26⅜	24¾	Travelers pfA		2.03	8.0	...	134	25⅜	25¼	25¼	+ ⅛
n	25¾	24⅜	Travelers pfE		2.00	7.8	...	328	25¾	25⅝	25⅝	− ⅛
	26⅜	24⅞	Travelers pfD		2.31	9.3	...	250	25	24⅞	24⅞	− ⅛
	89⅛	23	Travelers wt			...	...	83	88	84¾	87¼	+ 1¼
	26⅜	23⅝	TrvlrsP&C pfA		2.02	7.9	...	245	25⅝	25½	25½	...
	25¾	23⅝	TrvlrsP&C pfB		2.00	7.9	...	82	25⅜	25¼	25¼	− ⅛
	40¼	23⅛	TrvlrsProp A	TAP	.30	.8	29	1081	39⅛	38⅜	39	+ ⅜
	58	28¾	♣TredegarInd	TG	.32	.6	18	140	56	55⅛	55⅜	− ⅝
	45	30	♣Tremont	TRE		...	14	44	44¾	44⅝	44¾	...
	11	4⅜	TriPolyta	TPI		...	...	196	5⅞	5⅝	5¾	+ ⅛
	28½	22¼	♣TriContl	TY	3.59e	13.2	...	575	27¼	27	27¼	+ ⅛
	23⅝	10	♣Triarc A	TRY		...	dd	1310	22⅛	21⅜	21¾	− ⅝
s	47⅞	31⅝	♣Tribune	TRB	.64	1.4	20	2132	46¾	46	46⅛	− ⅝
	32¼	18	TrigenEngy	TGN	.14	.6	23	19	24⅜	24⅛	24⅛	− ¼
n	24¼	15⅜	TrigonHlthcr A	TGH		...	...	276	22⅜	22	22	− ¼
▲	30	19⅞	TriMas	TMS	.28f	.9	18	649	30½	30	30⅜	+ ⅜
	36¾	29	♣TriNetCp	TRI	2.52	7.6	16	656	33	32⅝	33	+ ⅜
n	26⅜	24	♣TriNetCp pfA		2.34	9.0	...	34	26	25⅞	26	...
n	26⅛	24⅝	♣TriNetCp pfB		2.30	9.0	...	24	25¾	25½	25⅝	...
s	34⅞	24⅛	TrinityInd	TRN	.68b	2.0	10	1386	34¼	32⅞	33½	− ⅞
	53⅞	32¼	♣TritonEng	OIL		...	cc	1669	45	44½	44⅞	+ ⅛
n	31¾	20⅞	TriumphGp	TGI		...	...	50	27⅛	26½	26½	− ⅝
	24⅞	12⅛	♣TrizecHahn	TZH	.24f	1.1	cc	2199	22	21⅝	21¾	− ¼
	26½	16¾	TrueNoComm	TNO	.60	3.0	16	175	20	19¾	20	+ ⅛
	32⅝	8¼	TrumpHtls	DJT		...	...	2153	12⅛	11¾	11¾	− ⅜
	20¾	12¼	♣TucsonElec	TEP		...	4	406	14¾	14½	14⅝	+ ⅛
	8⅝	**4¼**	**♣Tultex**	**TTX**		...	**11**	**4355**	**6⅜**	**5⅞**	**6**	**− ⅜**
	55½	29⅞	Tupperware	TUP	.66e	1.7	15	2752	40⅜	39½	40	+ ⅛
	7½	4⅞	TurkishFd	TKF	.14e	2.3	...	110	6	5⅞	6	...
	22⅛	14½	20CentInd	TW	.15e	.7	23	214	22	21⅝	21⅞	+ ⅛
	25⅞	21⅜	TwinDisc	TDI	.70	2.7	9	60	25⅞	25½	25⅞	+ ½
x	13⅛	12⅛	2002TargetTrm	TTR	.86	6.6	...	45	13⅛	13	13	...
	67¾	35½	♣TycoInt	TYC	.20	.3	28	8142	67⅝	65⅞	67⅜	+ ⅝
	2¾	1⅜	TylerCp	TYL		...	dd	820	2¼	2⅛	2⅛	...
			-U-U-U-									
	81⅜	41½	UAL Cp	UAL		...	11	3416	75¾	74⅛	74¾	− ¼
	35⅛	32⅛	UAL Cp dep pfB		3.06	8.7	...	1	35	35	35	...
n	35	33½	UAL Cp Cap TOPrS		3.31	9.7	...	20	34¼	34⅛	34⅛	...
	49⅞	**32¼**	**UCAR Intl**	**UCR**		...	**14**	**4599**	**44**	**41**	**41**	**− 3⅛**
	25⅜	20⅞	UGI	UGI	1.44f	6.4	16	543	22¾	22⅝	22⅝	− ¼
	14⅝	7⅜	UNC	UNC		...	32	736	14⅝	14½	14½	...
s	43⅞	28⅜	UNUM	UNM	.57	1.3	23	3011	43⅞	43⅜	43⅞	+ ¼
	26⅝	25⅛	UNUM Mids	UND	2.20	8.3	...	74	26½	26⅜	26⅜	...
	12⅞	7	URS Cp	URS		...	12	60	12	11⅞	12	...
	39¼	22¾	USA WasteSvc	UW		...	...	11440	37	36⅝	36⅞	+ ⅛
	17¾	14½	US CanCp	USC		...	12	214	16	15⅜	15⅜	− ½
▲	23⅞	15	USF&G	FG	.28f	1.2	12	7892	24½	23¾	23⅞	+ ⅛
	38¾	25¾	♣USG	USG		...	41	1221	38⅛	37⅝	38	...
	23⅛	11½	♣USG wt			...	...	261	22⅜	22	22	− ¼
▲	52⅝	28⅞	USLIFE	USH	.99	1.9	24	1534	53	51⅞	52⅞	+ ¼
	9⅜	8¾	USLIFE Fd	UIF	.76a	8.4	...	6	9	9	9	...
	⅞	1/32	US 1 Ind	USO		...	...	2	5/16	5/16	5/16	− 1/32
	35⅜	25½	UST Inc	UST	1.62	5.5	12	5419	29⅝	28¾	29⅝	+ ⅛
	25⅝	23⅝	USX Cap MIPS A		2.19	8.7	...	24	25¼	25¼	25¼	...
	47¾	41⅜	USX pfA		3.25	6.9	...	56	47⅛	46½	47	+ ⅜

Source: Reprinted by permission of THe Wall Street Journal, © 1997 Dow Jones & Company, Inc.
All Rights Reserved worldwide.

Dividend

A dividend is a payment that a company makes to shareholders. Not all companies pay a dividend, therefore, this column may be blank. When a dividend figure is listed, it's the estimated dividend payment that a company would pay a shareholder over the course of the entire year. To determine the average amount the company pays per quarter (companies announce their earnings on a quarterly basis, so that's when shareholders usually get paid), it's necessary to divide this figure by four. Stocks that recently announced dividends are generally marked with an X in the stock tables, meaning the stock is "ex dividend." A shareholder must own the stock on the day the firm announces the dividend in order to receive the dividend for that quarter. If you own stock in a company that declares a dividend in any given quarter, you will receive a check in the mail for the dividend per share multiplied by the number of shares you own. For instance, if IntraWeb announced a quarterly dividend of $.15 a share, a stock owner with 50 shares would receive a dividend check of $7.50. The dividend column for IntraWeb would also list $.60; $.15 times four, an estimated dividend payout for the entire year.

Yield

The column usually next to the dividend listing is entitled "Yield" or "Yield %." This figure is a way to gauge what kind of return the dividend alone provides the investor in a uniform way. To find the dividend yield of stock, divide the current yearly dividend by the stock price. That percentage is the yield. For instance, if the stock price of IntraWeb was $45 and the company issued an estimated yearly dividend of $.60, the yield would be, 1.3 percent ($.60 divided by $45). Investors use the yield to compare the dividend returns of different stocks. The reason: One simply cannot compare dividends directly to determine which stocks pay a better return. For example, suppose different companies pay out an annual dividend of $2. If one stock trades at $50 and the other at $80, the former has a better yield (4 percent) and therefore provides more income per dollar of investment than the latter (2.5 percent).

> **This will not be on the test.** Talk about the real thing. If all the Coca-Cola ever produced was flowing over Niagara Falls, the massive water wonder would flow at its normal rate for about nine hours.
> Source: Coca-Cola Company

Volume

The volume is a measure of the number of shares of a particular stock which were traded on a given day. This number is expressed in hundreds of shares, so a stock that lists a volume of 600, actually means that 60,000 shares of that stock changed hands that day. The paper will make a notation if the number of shares listed is the actual number of shares traded. The bigger the stock, the bigger the volume. AT&T, for example, may have more than five million shares trading on a given day, whereas a smaller stock with just a handful of shareholders may only have a few hundred shares exchanged per day. One of the times when volume becomes an issue is when very few shares of a given stock are traded. Fewer traded shares may affect how easily a shareholder could unload his or her holdings when needed.

High, Low, Close, and Net Change

After everyday of trading, the newspaper includes the high, low, and closing prices of a stock. These three figures tell you what the highest and lowest prices of a stock were in the course of a given day, as well as the price the stock was at when the market closed that day. It's a mini-version of the 52-week high and low price change. For instance, the price of IntraWeb stock may have opened the day of trading at $25 1/2, gone up to $26 3/4, then down to $25, and finally ended at $26. The stock table therefore would list the high at $26 3/4, the low at $25 and the close at $26. It would also list the net change at 1/2. The net change is the difference between the closing price of the stock that day compared to the closing price from the previous trading session.

Beta

No relation here to the college fraternity, beta is a comparative measure of how a stock performs compared to the market as a whole. On the stock exchanges, a rising market, like a tide, tends to lift most stocks with it; a falling market tends to depress them. The financial experts have devised a way to measure just how close the correlation is. They call it "beta."

It's assumed that the market has a beta value of one—its movement is an exact replica of itself. Stocks may have a beta value of more or less than one. When a stock has a beta of more than one, say, 1.5, it means that when the market goes up or down, that stock is likely to go up or down 50 percent more than the market. For example, if the market rose 20 percent in a year, a stock with a beta of 1.5 would have risen about 30 percent, or approximately 50 percent more than the market's 20 percent rise. Similarly, if the market fell 10 percent, that stock would probably have fallen around 15 percent. On the other hand, if a stock has a beta of less than one, it will fluctuate less than the market as a whole. For instance, if a stock has a beta of 0.75, it will react 25 percent less extremely than the average ups and downs of the market. If the market rose 30 percent, a stock with a beta of 0.75 would rise about 22.5 percent. If the market fell 10 percent, that stock would likley fall 7.5 percent. Suppose that IntraWeb had a beta of 1.2. If the market climbed about 10 percent, IntraWeb would likely go up around 12 percent. If IntraWeb's beta was calculated at 0.8, a 10 percent rise in the market would only translate into an 8 percent rise for the stock. Incidentally, a stock with a negative beta tends to move in the opposite direction of the market.

Understanding the beta is useful when determining the volatility of a stock compared to the market as a whole. In general, high betas are good when the market is rising, but they can be brutal when the market is heading south. Conversely, betas less than one are better in bad markets–they don't drop as badly but don't gain as much in good markets.

Why care about betas anyway? After all, if conventional wisdom holds that stocks of good companies do well and stocks of bad companies perform poorly over time, the beta simply shouldn't matter, right? Unfortunately, it does. Some experts say the entire market dictates 70 percent of an individual stock's movement up or down (think tides again); the company's performance just 30 percent. So when an investor evaluates a given stock for his or her portfolio and wants to gauge how greatly the price might fluctuate, understanding the beta factor is wise.

Stock Splits

Stocks can trade at any price. Some small companies may trade for literally pennies a share. Others, like Berkshire Hathaway, a stock that's headed by investing legend Warren Buffett, trades for around $40,000 a share. Market forces of supply and demand usually dictate the price of a share, but the board of directors of a company can have some influence as well. The board may decide that the price of a share is either too high or too low for the type of investor they'd like to attract.

When it is decided that a stock price has become too high, the board may elect to offer a stock split, which can cut the price of the stock in half in the case of a 2-for-1 split. They may also elect for splits of 3-for-1, 4-for-1, 5-for-2, etc. To make up for the reduced price of stock in the case of a 2-for-1 split, the company doubles the

Broker: *A licensed person who acts as an intermediary between the individual and the exchange in buying and selling securities such as stocks. Brokers charge a fee for this service known as a commission.*

Full-Service Brokers	Web Address	Phone
A.G. Edwards	http://www.agedwards.com/	314-289-3000
Alex. Brown & Sons Inc.	http://www.alexbrown.com/	800-638-2596
Bear Stearns	http://www.bearstearns.com/	800-371-0978
Chase Securities		212-552-2301
Dean Witter	http://www.deanwitter.com/	800-240-3932
Goldman Sachs	http://www.gs.com/	800-323-5678
Kidder Peabody		800-552-7725
Merrill Lynch	http://www.ml.com/	212-449-1000
Paine Webber	http://www.painewebber.com/	800-964-0085
Prudential Securities	http://www.prusec.com/	800-266-6263
Smith Barney	http://www.smithbarney.com/	212-399-6000

Discount Brokers	Web Address	Phone
AccuTrade	http://www.accutrade.com	800-598-2635
Aufhauser	http://www.aufhauser.com	800-368-3668
Bull & Bear	http://www.networth.galt.com	800-847-4200
E*Trade	http://www.etrade.com	800-786-2575
Fidelity	http://www.fid-inv.com	800-544-5235
Lombard	http://www.lombard.com	800-566-2273
National Discount Brokers	http://www.ndb.com	800-888-3999
PC Financial Network	http://www.pcfn.com/	800-825-5723
Quick & Reilly	http://www.quick-reilly.com	800-634-6214
Charles R. Schwab	http://www.schwab.com	800-372-4922
Waterhouse Securities	http://www.waterhouse.com	800-775-1763
Jack White and Company	http://www.pawws.com	800-753-1700

number of shares outstanding so the value of any portfolio holding that stock remains constant. For example, suppose a shareholder owned 50 shares of IntraWeb stock that traded for $40 a share. If the board of that company declared a 2-for-1 split, the shareholder's number of shares would increase from 50 to 100 shares, but the price per share would drop from $40 to $20. The total worth of the stock owned by the shareholder does not change; in this case, it remains at $2000 before as well as after the stock split. On the stock tables, a stock which has announced it is going to split, or which recently split, is usually noted by an "S" next to the stock symbol.

There are numerous notations that newspapers use to chronicle the life of a stock. Like a map, newspapers have a key that explains what different symbols on the stock page indicate. Some newspapers, for instance, use bold face and underline fonts to indicate extraordinary circumstances of particular stocks, such as large price changes or particularly heavy trading. When in doubt, look at the beginning of the stock tables in the business section for clarifications and definitions.

Brokers and Commissions

There's little question among financial experts that short of buying your own home, stocks are the single best long-term investment an individual can make (one reason homes make better investments: you can live in them while they make money for you). Over most of this century, the stocks of well-run companies have produced some of the best returns of any investments.

But before plunging straight into stocks, it's important to understand one potential stock market obstacle: getting into the market. Buying stocks is not as simple as dropping into the neighborhood market to pick up a quart of milk. A group of intermediaries, called *brokers*, handle the actual transaction of buying and selling the stock, and their services are not free. Virtually everyone who buys and sells stocks on the market has to do so through a broker, except in special cases (to be discussed later).

In general, there are two kinds of brokers that one can employ to handle trades: full-service brokers and discount brokers. *Full-service brokers* work at some of the marquee-name firms of Wall Street, such as Merrill Lynch or Goldman Sachs. These brokers tend to charge investors a premium for transaction services because along with trades, they provide research, analysis, and predictions from the in-house group of stock-trackers. Some investors prefer paying extra for this service. These brokers can also be a good reality-check barrier for new investors who may hear a "hot tip" on a stock and rush to buy it without understanding the ramifications of doing so.

The second kind of brokers were born on May 1, 1975, when two major stock exchanges lifted their rules about how minimum commissions had to be charged. That "May Day," as it is known, ushered in a new kind of broker called the *discount broker.* As the name implies, discount brokers generally charge less (sometimes up to 70 percent less) for their services compared to a full-service broker. But as the saying goes, you get what you pay for. When using a discount broker like Charles Schwab or Quick & Reilly, the investor receives little or nothing in the way of analysis, advice, or predictions from the broker (upon request, some houses may provide third-party information about a particular stock). This, of course, is what some self-directed and independent investors want. When the market is doing well, more investors turn toward discount brokers with the understanding that they can make money without the need for professional advice or analysis. (It's when the market drops that advice from a broker is often sought for a premium.) For smaller investors, discount brokers can also be popular in that the commission rates don't eat into the entire would-be investment.

Although actual dollar amounts may vary, brokers' commission rates generally follow a pattern. Brokers, for instance, all charge a minimum price for a trade, maybe $15 or $29 for a discount broker. That means that whether an investor buys 10 shares or 100 shares of a stock such as, say, McDonalds, she or he would pay the same dollar amount of commission on the trade. What this translates into is that smaller transactions end up costing more in commissions on a percentage basis. Ironically, those who receive a single share of a company as a "gift" may find that selling that one share later often costs more than the value of the share itself. Nice present.

Consider the following chart taken from discount brokers Quick & Reilly (1-800-634-6214). The transaction amount refers to the total value of the stock purchased. Remember: All transactions are subject to a minimum charge of $37.50. The purchase of one share of McDonalds trading at $40 would cost $37.50 because of the commission minimum. Fifty shares of McDonalds trading at $40 a share would be calculated as follows: .014 x $2000 (50 x $40 = $2000 principal) + $22 = $28 + $22, for a total of $50 in commission fees.

Transaction Amount	Commission Rate
$0–2,500	.014 x principal + $22
$2,501–6,000	.0045 x principal + $38
$6,001–22,000	.0025 x principal + $59
$22,001–50,000	.0017 x principal + $77
$50,001–500,000	.00085 x principal + $120
$500,001+	.00068 x principal + $205

Source: Quick & Reilly

Opening an account (which you are required to do) with a brokerage house is similar to opening an account at a bank. Brokerage firms will ask for basic info—name, address, phone—as well as information about your employer. They will also ask for a deposit, often between $500 and $2000, to establish an account before you begin buying and selling. You can often mail in the form and check or electronically transfer this amount from your bank account to the brokerage house. The firm will then hold this money in a cash account (actually, a money market account which gains some interest credited to your account) while they wait for your orders. When you call them to buy a certain stock, they pull from this account the total cost of the stock plus the cost of the commission. Likewise, when you call to sell a stock or a stock declares a dividend that is not reinvested, they put these earnings into your account. You can withdraw from this account on demand after subtracting the commission costs. At all times this money is very accessible, but most brokers require that you maintain a minimum dollar balance either in stock value or in the cash account.

It's important to note that even as commission rates fall with discount brokers and online trading, frequent buying and selling can really eat into any returns, particularly for beginning investors. Consider the case of first-time investor Michael. After doing some research on various software company stocks, Michael decided to buy 100 shares of IntraWeb stock trading at $10 a share. In January, Michael opened an account with a discount brokerage (he had to establish a $2000 account before he could buy or sell any

Expert Corner

How to pick a broker or investment advisor. There are a number of sources to turn to for advice when choosing a financial professional: the recommendations of friends, family, others in the professional field, even financial journals that publish their top picks. However, it's vital that you feel comfortable with any broker or consultant you pick and that he or she understands your goals and values, particularly if you're dealing with a new portfolio size somewhere between lunch money and a week's salary. Robert Levitt, an investment advisor, based in Boca Raton, FL suggests asking a broker the following questions.

1. *What are your credentials and education?*
2. *What is your investment strategy?*
3. *What are your references?*
4. *Are you paid from worth or sales?*
5. *What is the minimum account size you work with?*
6. *What is the average account size you work with?*
7. *Do you primarily work with individuals or institutions?*
8. *What is your investment philosophy?*

stocks). He instructed the brokerage to purchase 100 shares of IntraWeb at the "market price," or the price that the stock was trading for on that particular day. The brokerage was able to purchase the 100 shares for him at $10 a share. Since the total portfolio value was $1000, the commission Michael was charged was the brokerage's minimum of $30, and his total cost for the transaction was $1030 for the stock. Ten months later, after a promising earnings report from IntraWeb drove the stock price up, Michael sold his 100 shares of the stock at $12 a share, hoping to end up with a 20 percent return in less than a year. The total value of this portfolio at that time was $1200 (100 shares @ $12 a share), which again the brokerage charged $30 to sell. A total of $1170 was put back into his personal brokerage account.

After the stock was sold, Michael did some math to verify his 20 percent investment return. His investment of $1030 had yielded $1170. However, upon closer inspection, Michael realized that the $140 dollars he had actually made was a return of only 14 percent, before taxes. Since he earned that profit on a stock he held less than one year, he would owe short-term capital gains tax, which might be higher than a long-term tax had he kept his money invested longer.

That means that while Michael had actually made a 20 percent return on this stock, the brokerage commissions ate away 6 percent of his return before taxes. This is one reason why small investors who buy and sell frequently to capture short-term growth end up squandering decent returns on commission charges and taxes.

How Stock Ownership is Listed

When a stock is purchased through a broker, the ownership of the shares may be listed in one of two ways. What is meant by "listed" is how the company issuing the stock keeps the names in their books. The first is in your name, the purchaser of the shares. If you bought Disney stock, for example, you would become the shareholder of record on Disney's books. The second way ownership of shares may be listed is in the name of the broker who purchased the shares for you. This is known as "street name," or in the name of the brokerage house. All records of your ownership are kept electronically and credited to your account. The company in which stock was purchased doesn't recognize you individually as the shareholder of record. Disney, in this example, would have no listing of you as the shareholder but would simply have the brokerage firm, such as Merrill Lynch or Charles Schwab, listed as the holder. Brokerage firms will usually default to having stocks placed in street name unless notified otherwise, because it's easier for them to manage accounts that way.

When purchasing shares, it's important to understand the benefits and drawbacks for each kind of listing. Although investors may end up with street-name accounts, it does carry some advantages. These include reduced paperwork and consolidated statements, especially when you own more than one company's stock. There's also no worry about protecting the fancy stock certificates from theft or damage. Furthermore, when the stock is kept in street-name, it's much easier for the brokers to sell the shares since they have all the necessary information in-house.

However, there are times when it's better to keep the shares registered in your own name. These include receiving stock freebies (discount hotel rates or free gum) and enrolling in certain stock purchase plans described next. If you wish to have a stock listed in your own name, you may request this at the time of purchase (and some firms may charge extra, since it's an extra service on their end), or you may have it done later, and again, a fee will probably be attached.

Cost-Cutting: Saying No to Brokers and Their Fees

Imagine being able to walk into a Wal-Mart to buy a couple cans of tennis balls, a new cooler, and 20 shares of the Wal-Mart stock. It seems farfetched, particularly after the generally-held "there's-just-no-way-around-these-guys" belief about brokers and commissions. A number of companies, however, are doing just that: offering their stock directly to individuals and bypassing the traditional role and fees of the broker altogether. Two such arrangements exist: Direct Stock Purchases and Dividend Reinvestment Plans (DRIPs).

Direct Stock Purchases

Dubbed "no-load stocks" by investing expert Charles Carlson, these plans enable individuals to purchase stock directly from a corporation without the help of a broker. The company handles all the paperwork and details, from sending out an application to giving regular updates on stock purchases.

How It Works

Currently, more than 320 companies (and that number seems to be growing) offer direct purchase plans. Most of these are larger, well-established companies like Exxon, Home Depot, and Procter &

Gamble. Investors who are interested in purchasing stock in one of these companies can call a toll-free number and request information and an application. After reading the material, an investor can open an account by mailing off a check for the minimum amount or more. After that, payments can be taken electronically and automatically from a savings or checking account each month to purchase more stock. This ends up being a similar arrangement to how mutual fund automatic payments work (described in Chapter 3).

Advantages of Direct Stock Purchase Plans

One of the best ways to invest overall is to do so regularly and consistently, known as dollar-cost averaging. Using this method–such as investing $100 a month every month–an investor will lower his or her overall cost per share by buying more shares when the price falls and less when it goes up (see Chapter 3 on Mutual Funds for more on this). By investing via a direct plan like the one described, an individual can easily and efficiently get the benefits of dollar-cost averaging. Most companies require small minimums to get started: $100, $50, even $25 for some. It should be noted that these direct stock purchase plans are not entirely free from charges. Investors may be charged a one-time set-up fee (around $10 or so), an annual maintenance fee, and a transaction fee (a basis rate plus a charge on the number of shares purchased). Not a joy, but these operating fees still remain lower than most brokerage commissions.

Another major advantage of direct stock purchases over regular stock is that these plans allow investors to buy fractional shares. In other words, if Wal-Mart stock was trading at, say, $42, a $100 stock purchase through a broker would be good for only two shares. The other $16 would go into a cash account or toward a broker's fee and not be invested. With a Wal-Mart direct purchase plan, the investor would purchase the two shares with $84 of the $100, plus the additional $16 would go toward the purchase of a third share, in this case 0.381 more shares. Over time, those fractional shares can add up, especially when dividends that often won't cover the purchase of a full share are reinvested. In addition, some companies will allow the purchase of new shares at a discount price below market value when dividends are reinvested.

Disadvantages

When investors study stocks for purchase, they may look at a number of different things including the share price. With direct purchase plans, investors lose the power to purchase stocks at a particular price on a particular date. The plans purchase shares for their customers on specific dates that, at times, may not be the best price to buy. Of course, with dollar cost averaging, this factor becomes less important over time, but it should be noted.

Another disadvantage with direct purchase plans involves selling. When selling stocks through a broker, an investor can place a call or an on-line request, and the sell transaction is executed almost immediately. With these plans, an investor must write a letter to the company requesting to sell the shares–a small disadvantage, for sure, but enough to be an extra time-consuming step.

Third, although many of the features of direct stock purchase plans mirror those of the mutual fund, it's important to remember that buying the stock of one company can be risky. If that stock takes a hit, the whole portfolio takes a plunge. That's a given in the market, but it's something that the investor needs to be aware of from the start.

This will not be on the test. If you managed to get through youth not doodling with Crayola crayons, you're not from this planet. Binney & Smith, the makers of those colorful wax sticks, say the average child in the United States will wear down 730 crayons by the time she or he is 10 years old. The company produces more than 2 billion crayons each year in 104 colors.
Source: Binney & Smith

To learn more about direct stock purchase plans, or to find out the most recent list of those companies offering these plans, check out the NetStock Direct Corporation's web site at *http://www.netstockdirect.com* or Charles Carlson's site at *http://www.DRIPinvestor.com*. Two other sites include: The Direct Investor (888-598-9890) *http://www.sdinews.org*, and No-Load Stock Insider (800-233-5922) *http://www.noloadstocks.com*.

Dividend Reinvestment Plans (DRIPs)

Similar to the direct stock purchase plans described above, dividend reinvestment plans (DRIPs) allow individuals to purchase stock directly from the company. Offered by about 1000 companies, DRIPs help investors make the most of compounding over time by putting every cent to work toward future growth. When a company issues dividends, the total amount an individual shareholder may receive is not worth much by itself. If you owned 10 shares of IntraWeb that recently declared a $.15 dividend per share, you'd receive a check for $1.50. But if that money is reinvested to buy more shares, it can start to add up over time. In addition to the shares purchased through reinvested dividends, most DRIPs also permit investors to make payments toward the purchase of more shares, often at a discounted rate of three to five percent, but possibly as high as 10 percent. Like the direct purchase plan, investors are allowed to purchase full and fractional shares, depending on the amount invested. Also similar is the fee structure, where an investor may pay a small set-up and maintenance fee determined by that company.

DRIPs have one big difference from direct purchase plans: In order to get started in a DRIP, an investor must already be a shareholder in the company. One share is sufficient to begin a DRIP, but this requires going through a broker and paying the accompanying commissions. In addition, the investor must be a shareholder on record to begin a DRIP. A stock held by the brokerage in street name is not sufficient.

Deep in the Heart of Taxes

As the saying goes, you can only be certain of two things in life: death and taxes. And with money made with investments, it's no different. In short, whenever an investor makes money on an investment like a stock, that person will eventually pay Uncle Sam (and your state government for that matter) for the honor. There are a lot of specifics to know about declaring income from investments, and it's a good idea to check a current tax reference book, an accountant, or the Internal Revenue Service to clarify any questions. Listed below are two of the more common tax liability issues that an investor will face when buying, selling, and owning stock.

Dividend Income

When a company in which an investor holds stock declares and pays out a dividend, that is taxable income. The company reports that dividend

PROFILE...

Chris Bubser, 32
Santa Monica, California
Like a lot of investors, Chris Bubser was interested in investing in stocks, but the level of commitment and discipline needed for success with the market was trying at times. "I was pretty good at the –Buy high, sell low– thing," she jokes. That's one reason Chris, a marketing manager at the bio-tech firm Amgen, joined an investment club in 1996. Investment clubs are similar to mutual funds in that a collection of people pool their money and selectively buy and sell stocks of their choice. In Chris's club, which consists of about 25 members, each person puts in $1000 to join the club, then an additional $150 per quarter. Her Los Angeles-based club meets once a month for dinner where members discuss new stocks to buy and current holdings to sell. Typically, a few members are asked to research a couple new stocks within a particular industry or sector at each meeting and present their findings to the club as a whole. The meetings are casual, but the stock decisions, as well as all book keeping, are extremely organized and professional, she notes (each member is given a thick collection of rules and by-laws that govern the club). As of early 1997, the club's holdings totaled more than $40,000, with each member holding an equal stake of about $1600. If you are interested in finding out more information about investment clubs or obtaining material on how to start your own, contact the National Association of Investors Corporation (NAIC) at (810) 583-6242 (http://www.better-investing.org/).

income not only to you (or your broker) but also to the IRS. When tax filing time comes around, an investor who received dividends will get a tax form known as a 1099-DIV—DIV is short for dividend— that notes exactly how much money was distributed in dividends during the previous fiscal year.

On the ubiquitous 1040 tax return form is a space allocated to dividend income (line 9, for you tax junkies). If the total dividend income received is less than $400, an investor can list the amount directly on the 1040. However, if this income is more than $400, the investor is required to submit with his or her return a separate Schedule B form which details that income more thoroughly. Regardless of which forms you are required to submit, you are not required to submit your 1099-DIV form with your return. The IRS receives a copy of this form directly from the company. The form you receive is for your own purposes or state tax purposes.

Capital Gains and Losses

Most investors hope that the stocks they own increase in value. After all "buy low, sell high" is the investing mantra, right? Here's the unfortunate catch though: Whenever stock prices increase in value and are sold for a profit, the investor will end up paying for it in taxes.

For starters, you don't have to pay taxes on a stock you own simply if the price, and subsequently the value of your portfolio, goes up unless you actually sell the shares for that increased price. Until that point, the gains are referred to as "unrealized," and the IRS doesn't take too much interest in them. But the minute you sell your shares and pocket a profit, you assume tax liabilities.

Once a stock is sold for a higher price than when it was purchased, that's known as a *capital gain.* Investors who sell for a gain will receive a form 1099 detailing the specifics of the sale, including the number of shares sold and total price of the transaction. Those figures must be reported on a tax form known as Schedule D, as well as listed on Form1040, line 13. If the selling price of the stock was lower than the purchase price, the investor has what's known as a capital loss. These are reported similarly to gains in that they must be listed on the same tax forms, but they actually work to reduce the overall tax liability that an investor would normally incur. It is perhaps one of the only good things that comes from not making money on stocks. Overall though, these are just two simplified stock sales and tax scenarios. There are a million and a half rules in the tax laws governing the sale of securities of stock, so it's important to read a guide or talk to an accountant if there are any questions.

Bonds

Chips and salsa. Penn & Teller. Stocks and bonds?

The financial press and investment professionals utter the phrase "stocks and bonds" as if these investments are siamese twins that have to be mentioned in the same breath. The fact is that the two types of investments are very different and should be regarded as means to fulfilling different goals.

Bond: A formal IOU ("certificate") from a corporation, the U.S. Treasury, or local governments to pay a debt—with interest—at a specified time ("maturity date"). Unlike stockholders, bond holders own only the debt, not a share of the corporation.

So What's a Bond Anyway?

Forget British secret agent 007. This type of bond is really a glorified IOU issued by a corporation, government, or some other agency. Unlike stocks, which signify partial ownership of a corporation, bonds represent buying into debt, like being a lender of cash. The investor acts like a bank: He or she gives a loan and gets paid interest in return until the loan, or bond, is repaid.

An investor buys a bond from an organization with the under-standing that the value, known as the principal (likely to be $1000), will be repaid at a specified time in the future. The investor makes money because the principal is repaid along with interest, a kind of thank you from the issuer for letting them borrow your money in the interim. The bondholder will either receive interest during the time before maturity, or in the case of what's called zero-coupon bonds, the investor receives it in the end when the bond matures.

How Is a Bond's Return Measured?

Like getting a loan for tuition or a new car, bonds come attached with a particular rate of interest. For example, if a bond paying 6 percent interest is purchased for its face of $1000, the investor will receive a yearly income of $60. A simple 6 percent return. Here's the catch, though, and it's something called yield.

Bonds, like other securities, are traded under the influence of the market's supply and demand forces. Suppose that when that bond paying 6 percent was first issued, the prevailing market interest rate was also 6 percent. The bond is on par with what other savings instru-ments are paying on the market. Suppose, however, that market inter-est rates increase to 7 percent while the bond is still paying just 6 per-cent. Since the bond is not quite as attractive as it once was, the face value would drop in value as investors would clamor for higher-paying bonds.

This interest rate factor will drive the return, or current yield, of the bond up or down during its term until maturity. This impact can be seen in the following example. Suppose a 10-year bond paying 6 percent interest is purchased for $1,000. Over the

The current yield on a particular bond is deter-mined by:

Annual Interest
———————
Price

How Bonds Are Rated

Like a new car might be rated by an independent third party for durability, quality, and reliability, bonds are similarly rated on their strengths. The two biggest groups that rate bonds are Standard & Poor's and another investment service called Moody's. Using slightly differing lettering sequences, both groups rate the bonds on the likelihood that the issuer will repay the loan in full at maturity. Anything with a rating of BB/Ba or lower is considered a junk bond.

Standard & Poor's	Moody's	What it means
AAA	Aaa	Best overall rating
AA	Aa	High rating
A	A	Good
BBB	Baa	Medium
BB	Ba	Slight default risk

Source: Standard & Poor's and Moody's Investment Services

decade-long life of the bond, the owner would receive a total of $600 in interest ($60 a year for 10 years) if held to maturity. Thus the yield could be determined by dividing the annual interest, in this case $60 by the price of the bond, $1000, equally 6 percent. Suppose the face value of that same bond dipped in price and is now selling for $900. Because of the decrease in the bond's price, the yield would increase. This bond would still be paying annual interest payments of $60, but the divisor would now be $950, pushing the yield up to 6.31 percent.

When an investor purchases a bond, he or she knows exactly what will be earned in interest on the investment. Because of this, bonds are referred to as a fixed-income security. This differs markedly from stocks, in which the investor doesn't know for sure whether dividends will be declared during the next quarter or whether the stock price will rise or fall. Bonds, however, require that the investor assume some risk. This type of risk involves not knowing how the bond will fare against inflation and interest rates (interest rate risk) or whether the firm issuing the bond will be financially sound enough come maturity to repay the principal (credit risk).

Interest Rate Risk

Bonds are issued with a number of built-in features, including the date of maturity and how much it will pay along the way. The latter, known as the interest on the bond, is fixed when the bond is purchased. The interest rate tells the investor exactly how much he or she will receive over the life of the bond. This could be anywhere from a few years to three decades. Of course, that presents a dilemma for the investor: getting trapped at one interest rate when the market rate may change. For example, if a 10-year bond is issued paying 7 percent interest, that return would be favorable if the going market rate was just 5 percent. But suppose later the market rate jumps to 9 percent.

TYPES OF BONDS

Bonds can be issued by a variety of groups, from Uncle Sam to General Electric to the New Jersey Transit Authority. Each of these bonds possesses special characteristics related to the issuer. For example,

U.S. Government: To pay off the public debt and fund operations, the U.S. Government auctions off three types of issues Treasury bills, notes, and bonds. Bills mature the fastest, often between nine days and one year, and are sold in denominations of $10,000. Notes can be purchased in denominations of $1000 and $10,000 and may have a maturity of from one to ten years. Bonds have the longest maturity dates (more than 10 years) and can be bought in $1000 and $10,000 denominations. Because these issues are backed by the full faith and credit of the United States government (Read: taxes), they are considered a risk-free investment and therefore pay less in interest than comparable corporate bonds, which carry some additional risk.

Corporate: Sold (known as "floating") by firms to raise capital for business expenditures, corporate bonds pay a rate of return based on the length of time until maturity and the financial strength of the firm. The lower the financial credibility of the firm and the more distant a maturity date, the higher the interest a firm will have to pay to attract investors.

Municipal: Also called "munies," these bonds are issued by local governments or agencies, like state highway departments. Municipal bonds typically pay less in interest than other bonds, but there's a reason. Interest from munies is exempt from federal taxes and is usually exempt from state and local taxes if the investor lives in the state that issued the bond.

That means the investor is left holding a bond paying interest two points below market, and is losing out on interest over a long time. And here's the bigger problem: If the investor wanted to dump that bond for one paying a higher rate, the principal (the amount paid for the bond), would have dropped in value as well, because the demand for a less-than-market-rate bond is not going to be heavy. An investor has the option to hold the bond until maturity to recover the entire amount of the principal, but by then he or she may have lost revenue from years of noncompetitive interest payments.

Credit Risk

When a corporation, government, or agency issues a bond, they're really saying, "Give us your money now, and we'll pay you back everything in the future, in addition to interest payments along the way." But what would happen if that government or company went belly-up in the time between issuing the bond and the date of its maturity? That's a credit risk that investors accept when purchasing bonds–one that the issuing group is aware of as well.

In general, the safer the group issuing the bond, the higher the bond is rated (see chart on previous page). When a stable group issues a bond, they may offer a particular interest rate. But when a less secure entity issues a bond, it usually has to offer a higher rate of return, or interest rate, to attract investors who demand more in return for assuming that risk. For instance, if a company teetering on bankruptcy was issuing bonds, it would have to cough up a higher interest rate than another company much more financially secure. Such bonds issued by groups that offer a higher-return, or yield, are commonly referred to as "junk bonds."

Q.u.i.c.k. D.o.w.n.l.o.a.d.

- Stocks represent ownership in a corporation. Companies issue stock to raise money to fund the expansion of this business. Investors purchase stocks to make money from the company as it grows and profits.

- Stocks can make money for their investors in one of two ways. The first is through dividends, which are profits distributed to shareholders. The second is when the price of a share increases, or appreciates, on the stock market and then is sold by the investor for that greater amount. This is known as a capital gain.

- The price of a stock may increase for any number of reasons. These can include: The company is performing well and profits are up; the firm just announced a new, superior product on the market; the market as a whole is doing well; or the firm is being bought out by another firm for a higher price per share.

- Stocks are bought and sold on exchanges. Exchanges are either actual organized places or computer-based networks where buyers and sellers of stock meet to trade. The oldest and largest exchange in the world is the New York Stock Exchange on Wall Street.

- Stock market indexes are collections of stocks used to track the movement of the stock market as a whole, or of a particular section of the market such as small-value stocks. Indexes can vary in the number and types of stocks they contain. The most famous index is the Dow Jones Industrial Average, which is comprised of 30 stocks on the New York Stock Exchange. When the market is said to be "up" or "down," this is usually a reference to the movement of the Dow.

- There are a plethora of definitions and concepts surrounding stocks. Some of the more frequently used ones include: 52-week high and low, P/E ratio, dividend, yield, volume, beta, and stock splits.

- Investors can obtain information on companies from a number of sources. One is the annual report, a publication produced by a company itself every year, that details the past operations of the business and its future goals. Another excellent resource is *Value Line Investment Survey*, a comprehensive manual on major stocks. It's available at most libraries in the reference section.

- Unlike basic goods and services, stocks generally cannot be purchased directly. Instead, investors must go through licensed professionals called brokers. There are two basic categories of brokers: full-service and discount. Full-service brokers provide investors with analysis, recommendations, and advice, and charge a premium for their services. Discount brokers offer little or nothing in the way of research or recommendations, but charge much less than full-service brokers. The type of broker that's best for an investor depends on his or her knowledge and experience with stocks.

- In addition to brokers, there are two additional ways in which an investor may buy into stocks. The first is through what's called a dividend reinvestment plan (DRIP), in which dividends from that company are automatically used to purchase new shares of stock directly through the company itself. The second is through what's been dubbed "no-load stocks." These are stocks that an individual may purchase directly from the company itself, bypassing the broker. Currently, about 150 companies offer such plans. More information on these plans can be found by calling the company's investor relations department directly.

- Investors have to pay taxes on stocks whenever they receive income or make a profit on the sale of the stock. Income may come in the form of dividends, which may be sent out quarterly. Investors are only liable for taxes when they sell their shares. The increase of a stock price alone does not require an investor to pay taxes, only when those shares are sold.

- A bond is a glorified IOU issued by a corporation, government, or some other agency. Unlike a stock, which is a stake in the ownership of a company, the bond represents a purchase into that firm's or government's debt.

- Bond investors pay a certain amount for the bond, known as the principal. After a specified amount of time, called the term, that principal is repaid along with interest. Both the interest rate and the term are established when the bond is purchased. Since these amounts, and therefore the income, are preset, a bond is known as a fixed-income security.

- There are two types of risk associated with bonds. Interest rate risk is the chance that the interest rate paid by the bond will drop below the overall market interest rate. It makes the bond less valuable. The second risk is financial risk. This is the gamble that the firm issuing the bond will not be solvent come maturity time and be able to pay back the principal of the bond.

3 From Mosh Pits to Mutual Funds

And if you listen now you might hear a new sound coming in as an old one disappears.–World Party*

Music Funds

Funk, jazz, rock, country, hip-hop. Nearly everyone likes music in one form or another. But when it comes to the hassles, like keeping up with new releases and reviews of your favorite bands, dealing with crowded stores trying to grab a hot new disc, or pouring over bins of used CDs looking for an older, obscure group, that's hardly music to anyone's ears. So unless, between the job or school, you have tons of time to commit to this endeavor, it can be a real challenge to keep up with the world of music.

Mutual Fund: An investment company that pools the money of many different individuals and invests it in stocks, bonds, and other securities under the guidance of a professional manager.

Now imagine that there was a service which, for a small fee, would do all that hassle-laden dirty work. This service–managed by a knowledgeable music buff who knows your tastes–would not only deal with the headaches of sifting through new releases of bands you like but also

*"Put the Message in a Box," written by Karl Wallinger, Copyright©1990 PolyGram Music Publishing, Ltd. Used by Permission. All Rights Reserved.

recommend other bands that fit your taste for you to sample. All the while you could spend your free time doing as you wish–playing sports, reading, or just veging in front of the tube. The service would also keep track of which music you owned and would send you a regular update categorizing your holdings.

Sound appealing? This is the basic idea of a mutual fund, only swap music fans with investors and the CDs and tapes with stock, bonds, and other securities. Mutual funds are companies that pool the money of many different individuals and invest their cash into stocks, bonds, and other securities under the guidance of a professional manager. Mutual funds benefit the individual investor who lacks the time and money to successfully delve into individual stocks and bonds, which can be a full-time job. After all, while you might be able to devote some spare time researching the right stocks or bonds to determine where to place your money, mutual funds are managed by professionals who do this kind of stuff for a living. The result: Mutual funds provide a simple, low-maintenance, cheap way (many require just $50 to open an account) to get into investing.

A Short Background

Despite their recent hype, the earliest mutual funds actually date back more than 70 years; the first fund was introduced in Boston in 1924. More recently, however, mutual funds have undergone explosive growth in the number of shareholder accounts, total assets, and the total number of funds available. The reasons for this increased presence are numerous, but most stem from the benefits they provide their owners and their ease of use. Another reason for their phenomenal growth is the number of Americans who have retirement savings through work invested in mutual funds.

The number of mutual fund accounts was around 140 million in 1996, up from about 40 million just a decade ago. At the same time, the number of funds on the market jumped from 1528 in 1985 to over 6000 today (see chart). That's nearly double the number of stocks on the New York Stock Exchange. Of course, this popularity has a downside: Picking a good fund among the thousands available is that much trickier. But before getting to the question of selecting a good fund–and more important, one that's right for you–it's necessary to understand just how mutual funds really work.

Year	Number of Funds
1985	1528
1986	1840
1987	2317
1988	2715
1989	2917
1990	3105
1991	3427
1992	3850
1993	4558
1994	5357
1995	5761
1996	6293

Source: *1997 Mutual Fund Fact Book*, Investment Company Institute, Washington, DC.

What Makes Mutual Funds Tick?

A mutual fund company pools together the money of many individuals and invests it into stocks, bonds, or other securities based on the objective, or goal, of the fund. That objective, which is determined by the management of the fund, can vary dramatically. Some funds may look to increase their overall value for shareholders by investing in young, start-up companies with great potential for growth. Others might place their money into more stable, established companies with a long history of solid growth and dividend payments. And still other funds may plow their money overseas into the Pacific Rim, Europe, or Latin America, looking for companies that might be strong growth contenders in the future.

Buying a mutual fund is similar to buying stock in a particular company in that you are actually buying mutual fund "shares" and thus making yourself a shareholder in that fund. Unlike stocks, however, which signify direct ownership in a company, mutual fund shares represent ownership of a fund, which in turn is invested into dozens, even hundreds, of stocks and bonds of different companies. In other words, if a particular mutual fund has purchased stock in Microsoft, Coca-Cola, Disney, and other companies, a shareholder in that fund is essentially an indirect stockholder in all of those companies, but without the rights usually afforded corporate shareholders. The vast majority of mutual funds on the market are what are called "open-ended" funds, meaning they have an unlimited number of shares the public can buy. However, there are a small number of funds known as "closed-ended" funds. Similar to stocks, closed-ended funds offer a limited number of shares upon inception of the fund. Those shares are then traded on the stock exchange just like a stock, and no further shares are issued.

NAV: Or net asset value, is the price of an individual share of a mutual fund. It's found by taking the total assets of the fund and dividing by the number of shares outstanding.

How Mutual Fund Shares Work

Prices of stocks move up and down daily based on the good old Adam Smith-inspired theory of supply and demand. Open-ended mutual fund shares work somewhat differently. The price of a mutual fund share, known as the net asset value (NAV), goes up or down, depending upon the value of the holdings of the fund. In other words, if all the assets of the fund (those Microsoft, Coca-Cola, and Disney shares, for example) were added together and then divided by the number of mutual fund shares outstanding, minus expenses, the NAV would be that amount. The NAV, in turn, would move up or down daily, depending on the value of all the investments of the mutual fund. If the value of most or all of the fund holdings went up on a given day, the NAV would rise. If most or all the holdings dropped, the NAV would fall.

HOW CAN AN OPEN-END FUND BE CLOSED?

Imagine if you were a fund manager assigned the duty of selecting and investing in new stocks and bonds for your fund's shareholders. Now imagine if you were very successful in your efforts, and the return of your funds proved popular among the investing public. Day in and day out, new money keeps coming in as new investors sign on to buy shares. You, in turn, find yourself in the difficult situation of picking more and more new stocks in which to place your shareholders' money (Funds, incidentally, are prohibited from putting more than 5 percent of their assets into any one security. This is a protection mechanism to make sure the fund is not banking too much on any one investment). Over time, the task of picking new stocks that meet your exacting standards becomes increasingly difficult. This might be especially true if your fund's objective limits the kinds of stocks in which money may be invested in the first place (some funds, for example, may invest in the stock of small companies in Latin America where there simply may not be that many). In a case like this, the fund's manager can opt to close the fund as a way to keep excess new money from pouring in. When a fund is closed, current shareholders are allowed to keep contributing money (and often enjoy the fund's good fortunes), but new shareholders are prohibited from jumping on board until the fund is reopened. How long a fund remains closed is at the discretion of the firm's management and may last from months to years. In the investing world it's very much like attempting to eat out at a restaurant but finding out that it is full and that you did not make reservations.

Suppose a hypothetical mutual fund, which we'll call the New Vision fund, has exactly $5 million in assets at the close of trading on Tuesday and exactly one million shares outstanding, the NAV that day would be $5. If you owned five shares of this fund, your shares would be worth $25. If on Wednesday, the holdings of the New Vision fund went up to $5.5 million and the number of shares remained constant at one million, the NAV would grow to $5.50 and your shares would be worth $27.50. Likewise, if the total value fell to $4 million, while the number of shares remained at one million, the NAV would dip to $4, and so on.

How mutual funds make money for investors

Mutual funds make money for their investors in a few different ways. The first is when the holdings of a fund itself increase in value and are sold by the fund manager for a profit, known as a capital gain. That income is passed onto the investor in the form of a "distribution." The second way to make money is when stocks or bonds held by the fund produce income either as a result of dividends (from stocks) or interest (from bonds). These distributions can either be received as cash or reinvested to purchase more shares of the fund. A final way a shareholder can make money with a mutual fund is when the NAV increases, and the shares are then sold off at that increased price. This produces another capital gain.

This point is both important and confusing, because most products in the marketplace, as a rule, seem to go up when demand increases (the price of downhill skis increases just before the ski season, not after it). In the case of mutual funds, demand for a particular mutual fund will not necessarily drive up the NAV as it would normally drive up a regular company stock. For example, suppose the New Vision fund received some good press and was written up in several investing journals as being the fund to own because of solid returns and its skillful fund manager. If interested investors flocked to the fund, buying another $5 million worth of shares and doubling it's total value, the NAV wouldn't necessarily increase. Why? That influx of cash added to the fund also added to the total number of

shares, keeping the NAV in check. This is one reason many journalists who cover the investment industry are allowed to own mutual funds: They can't drive up the price for personal gain (as they might be able to do with an individual stock they reported on favorably). The value of a mutual fund goes up only when the holdings of that mutual fund increase in value.

Another distinction between mutual fund shares and regular stock shares is how they are issued. Except in special cases, when investors purchase stock in a company, they usually purchase full shares of the stock, 25, 44, or 110 shares, for example. With mutual funds, on the other hand, an individual can purchase full shares or fractions thereof. For example, suppose an investor decided to purchase $500 worth of the New Vision fund on a day the NAV was trading at $12.75. If this were regular stock trading at the same price, he or she would be able to purchase exactly 39 shares, with a little of the $500 left over. However, if it were a mutual fund, that same investor would be able to purchase roughly 39.22 shares of the fund. This is possible because mutual funds pool the money of many different investors, allowing the managers to buy full shares, in turn, of stock. The shares the investor has purchased are simply shares of the larger pool of funds. The individual is therefore able to own fractional share amounts, in this case 0.22 worth.

Advantages of Mutual Funds

There are a number of advantages mutual funds have over other kinds of investments, particularly for new investors just starting out with only a few bucks. Among the biggest benefits of mutual funds to beginning investors are:

Diversification: One of the major benefits of mutual funds is that they allow new investors, even those starting with just a few dollars, to enjoy the benefits of portfolio diversification. Diversification means that the investor's money is divided between many different types of stocks and bonds, allowing the investor to cushion losses from a single investment. Many personal finance experts suggest you need roughly $10,000 (on the very low end) to properly diversify your portfolio in stocks to buffer against loss. Unless you have that kind of money to diversify investment holdings on your own, mutual funds provide a means to instant diversification with a minimal amount of money.

Professional Management: Mutual funds are run by a fund manager. When you purchase a mutual fund, you also hire the expertise of a fund manager (and their research staff) whose full-time job is to eat, drink, and sleep mutual funds. The fund manager looks over the fund's portfolio, choosing when to execute the trades, how much of a particular stock to own, etc., all of which affects the worth of the fund. Fund literature and other sources, like investment magazines, are often good for researching a fund manager, including its investment strategies and past performances.

Ease of Investment: You're probably busy and don't want to deal with daily or weekly investment decisions. With mutual funds, investors don't need to. By using something called automatic payment systems (when a mutual fund company automatically deducts a preset amount of money from your bank account each month) and taking

---

Four reasons why mutual funds are smart investments for young investors:

1. **Diversification:** Allows investors starting with only a few dollars to spread their money over a wide range of stocks and bonds–a typically expensive process–to protect against losses.
2. **Professional Management:** Allows inexperienced investors the benefit of professional managers who eat, drink, and sleep investing.
3. **Ease of Use:** Mutual funds offer hassle-free options, like automatic deposit, and cheap start-up costs.
4. **Cost Controls:** Unlike stocks, which require brokers and their commission charges to get started, many funds can be started without such fees.

advantage of cheap start-up costs, young investors can get started in mutual funds for as little as $50.

Cost Controls: One of the challenges for new investors is getting started without getting killed by all the fees and charges normally associated with the trade. With mutual funds, particularly no-load mutual funds, investors can often avoid such charges.

A Closer Look at This Cost Thing

Mutual funds have one distinct advantage over stocks and bonds: cost. That's because when you buy and sell stocks directly, you usually have to pay a commission charge to a broker. And these are charges that an investor pays both when buying and selling a stock. For someone investing just a few hundred dollars, those commissions can really eat into returns. Consider this: Suppose $500 were invested in a NYSE stock. The commission of a discount broker rate might be $29 per transaction (buying and selling counted separately). That means even before a single return can be calculated from the stock's performance, $58 dollars, or 11.6 percent of the total value would effectively be deducted.

Load: *A sales charge paid by shareholders when buying (known as a front-end load) or selling (called a back-end load) a mutual fund.*

With some mutual funds, there are fees called loads. A load, like a commission, is a sales charge that an investor pays when buying or selling a mutual fund. If the load is charged when the fund is purchased, it's called a "front-load." If it's paid when selling shares, it's called a "back-end" or "redemption" fee. Either way, these can be killers. For example, if you invested $500 in a fund that charged a 4 percent front-end load (loads typically run from 3 to 8.5 percent, depending on the fund), you would only in fact be investing $480; $20 would be skimmed off the top. Each subsequent purchase made into the fund would also be reduced by the amount of the load. It's not too hard to figure out that these kinds of charges can really add up over time and diminish your returns.

Enter no-load funds. A no-load fund is a mutual fund with no sales charge. This means that when $500 is invested, $500 is actually invested. These funds often avoid charging a load to the investor by selling the fund directly to the investor through a discount service or directly over the phone. Like buying a stereo or computer wholesale, avoiding the middle-person's markup, no-load funds enable you to reduce the costs associated with owning a fund. While they may not charge any kind of fee up front, note that all funds still have to pay for their expenses and will charge you what's called an "administrative" or "management fee." This is usually only a percentage point or two and will only appear as a slight reduction in the NAV. A fund may also charge the investor through another fee system called 12b-1 charges. These charges (named for the Securities and Exchange Commission code section from which they were created) are used to pay promotion and marketing costs of the fund, and may at times be pricy. So when perusing the various funds available, even no-load funds, be sure to check the total expenses listed under management fees or 12b-1 charges.

> **No-Load Fund:**
> A mutual fund that does not impose a sales charge, or load, when it's bought or sold by the investor.

Fund Objectives

After assessing your own investment objectives, risk tolerance, and time horizon, it's important to find an investment instrument that matches those needs. Over the years, mutual funds have been broken into different categories, based upon their objectives and investment strategies. This was done in an attempt to help organize the funds as the numbers on the market exploded. It also helps investors compare how a fund is doing versus other funds in the same category. The different categories of funds allow the investor to understand what the fund manager is trying to accomplish and get a sense of what kinds of stocks, bonds, or other securities the fund will be investing in to achieve that goal.

> **12b-1 Fee:** Different and often in addition to loads, this is an annual mutual fund sales charge levied on investments for promotion and marketing costs in the fund. Its numeric name comes from the Securities and Exchange Commission rule that allows funds to charge the fee.

AVERAGE ANNUAL RETURNS

Objective	1-Yr (%)	5-Yr (%)	10-Yr (%)	15-Yr (%)	20-Yr (%)
Aggressive Growth	7.02	12.53	11.55	13.87	14.94
Growth	17.65	13.51	11.98	15.29	15.39
Growth and Income	22.02	14.54	11.62	14.90	13.80
World Stock	14.99	11.24	9.80	14.75	14.65
Corporate Bond	5.36	7.19	8.08	11.45	9.37
Government Bond	4.04	5.77	6.77	9.90	8.82

Returns through 2/28/97
Source: Morningstar Mutual Funds

Knowing this allows the investor to understand the types of risk associated with that kind of mutual fund.

There are multiple ways in which mutual funds can be categorized and organized based on the holdings of the fund and its financial objectives. This sounds simple enough, but the titles and categories differ by groups such as those that manage the funds and those that track them. The following contains some of the more prevalent types of funds as noted by the mutual fund trade group, the Investment Company Institute in Washington, DC.

This will not be on the test. If you think the world is being taken over by Starbucks and its loyal legion of coffee swillers, take heart. In 1996, the per capita consumption of coffee was 1.7 cups a day, down some 45 percent from the 3.1 cups level in 1962.
Source: National Coffee Association

Stock Funds

Agressive Growth Funds: These funds seeks to maximize growth in capital with little priority given to current income, such as dividends. Both the portfolio itself, such as smaller, new companies, and the investment techniques, may entail extra risk. They are typically considered one of the highest-risk categories of funds.

Growth Funds: Invest in the common stock of well-established companies. These funds seek capital growth with just a small emphasis on current income.

Growth and Income Funds: These funds invest in companies that can increase in value but also have an established record of paying dividends. Equal emphasis on current income and future growth. Considered moderate-risk funds.

Global Funds: Invest mostly in the stocks of companies that are traded globally, including the United States. Both global and international funds seek capital growth in the value of their investments.

International Funds: Invests in the stocks of companies that are strictly located overseas.

Income-Equity Funds: Invests in companies with high dividend-paying stocks. The primary goal of these funds is to generate a high level of income.

Exactly what are "Index Funds" and should you invest in them?

"It's hard to beat the market," financial experts like to say. What they mean by "beat the market" is to selectively pick a portfolio of stocks that produce a higher return than all stocks as a whole. So if you can't beat 'em, join 'em, right? This is the thinking behind index funds. Unlike actively managed funds where a manager decides into which stocks the fund's money will be placed, index funds invest their cash into a preset collection of stocks. These stocks usually mirror a market index of some kind like the Standard & Poor's 500 (a collection of 500 major stocks on the New York, American and over-the-counter stock exchanges) or the Wilshire 5000 Equity Index (a compilation of all stocks listed on the NYSE, AMEX and widely-traded OTC issues).

The all-important question, though, is whether you should invest in an index fund? Although experts differ on the issue, many seem to say go with index over actively managed funds. Although investing in index funds means you'll never beat the market, these funds are a strong choice for two reasons. First, they tend to beat most actively managed funds in short- and long-term returns (some studies suggest they beat up to 75 percent of all fund managers). Second, because they buy and hold stock in preset companies, there's less trading of shares that an active manager might do, which helps keep the operating costs (such as commissions) and taxable income of the shares lower. Several mutual funds companies offer index funds, including Fidelity (800-544-8888) and Vanguard (800-635-1511). Vanguard's Index 500 Fund is especially popular, counting over $40 billion in assets in 1997, making it, overall, the second largest mutual fund.

Bond Funds

Balanced Funds: A mixture of stocks and bonds, these funds look to preserve the value of principal, but also earn some current income and achieve some long-term growth.

Global Bond Funds: Invest in debt securities in companies and countries worldwide, including the United States.

Corporate Bond Funds: Invests primarily in the the debt of American corporations and seeks a high level of income.

Municipal Bond Funds: Invest in bonds issued by state and municipal governments. This income, unlike regular bond interest income, is exempt from federal taxation.

U.S. Government Income Funds: Invest in a number of government securities including U.S. Treasury bonds and seeks current income through interest payments.

Money Market Funds

Taxable Money Market Funds: Invests in short-term, high-quality securites such as certificates of deposit and Treasury bills. It seeks to maintain a stable net asset value, usually $1 a share.

Tax-Exempt Money Market Funds: Invest in securities that are exempt from federal taxes and in special cases state taxes for residents of that state.

Picking a Mutual Fund That's Right For You

The next big step is compiling of list of candidate funds that might be right for you, based on your investment objectives. So before tearing the mutual fund listing from the paper and tacking it to the dart board, here are a few questions and considerations to be addressed:

- Why do you want to invest, and when do you plan on using this money (i.e., saving for a new laptop, law school, a new house, or retirement)?

- How risk-tolerant or risk-aversive are you with investments?

- How much money are you able to start with and contribute regularly?

Each fund category has a particular risk and return curve that needs to be thoroughly understood before proceeding. Once you've determined your investment needs (e.g., a down payment on a house in 10 years), it's possible to start narrowing down the choices of which funds may be right for you.

Researching and Finding Mutual Funds

Along with the recent explosion in the number of funds, there's been a parallel explosion in the number of sources to get information on various funds, ranging from newsletters and journals to lots of Internet and Web Sites.

For published data, there are several excellent sources to research mutual funds, how they've performed, and what they cost to begin. *The Wall Street Journal, Barron's* and *Kiplinger's Personal Finance Magazine* are three, but the grand-daddy of mutual fund info is a publication called *Morningstar*. A veritable Bible of mutual funds, the Chicago-based *Morningstar* lists thousands of funds, along with cost, returns, management, objective, size in assets, and how well each compares with other funds within its category. Found in the reference section of most libraries, *Morningstar* also ranks funds on its own one- to five-star scale. There is a veritable plethora

<Online Info>

In addition to the fund families on the Web, there are also sites that enable investors to bone up on mutual funds jargon, compare returns, and research new funds—all for free. Two of the better ones are:

Mutual Funds Magazine
http://www.mfmag.com/start.htm
A family of tools for researching and evaluating mutual funds. Among the offerings: Hundreds of stories and thousands of historical charts.

The Mutual Fund Investor's Center
http://www.mfea.com/
A plethora of helpful information, including a comprehensive index of thousands of funds and the basics of how to read a prospectus.
</Online Info>

of mutual fund investing info available online (a simple query of "mutual funds" brought up 743,374 related sites on Infoseek, and that number appears to be growing daily). Listed below are some of the better sites with mutual funds information, including some of the bigger fund families and their contact information.

Can You Afford a Mutual Fund?

All right, you've done your homework on finding a few good funds, you've determined your risk level, and you've decided what you're investing for in the first place. But now comes the moment of truth: Can you afford it? At first glance, the answer may seem to be a resounding no, owing to the "minimum payment" requirement listed for many funds. This starting amount can often be listed at $1000, $2500, even $10,000.

Volume 29, Issue 6, January 31, 1997. Reprinted with permission.

FPA Capital

	Ticker	Load	NAV	Yield	SEC Yield	Assets	Mstar Category
	FPPTX	Closed	$34.01	0.9%	—	$492.9 mil	Small Value

Prospectus Objective: Small Company

FPA Capital Fund seeks long-term growth of capital. Current income is secondary.

The fund invests in common stocks, preferred stocks, and convertible securities of small- and medium-size companies that the advisor believes to be undervalued. In selecting investments, the advisor considers a company's profitability, book value, replacement cost of assets, and free cash flow. The fund may invest up to 10% of assets in foreign issues.

The fund closed to new investors on July 1, 1995.

Historical Profile										
Return	High									
Risk	Above Avg	95%	96%	96%	96%	93%	92%	79%	74%	
Rating	★★★★									
	Highest									

Investment Style
Equity
Average Stock %

Growth of $10,000
▓ Investment Value $000 of Fund
— Investment Value $000 S&P 500
▼ Manager Change
▽ Partial Manager Change
— Mgr Unknown After
◄ Mgr Unknown Before

Performance Quartile (within Category)

History				1990	1991			2-01	
11.41	11.08	11.74	12.46	13.89	10.91	16.96	18.89	20.06	20.61	27.50	34.01	NAV
28.95	12.57	10.97	18.11	25.25	-13.80	64.51	21.57	16.74	10.37	38.39	37.76	Total Return %
-2.78	-6.11	5.71	1.50	-6.43	-10.68	34.03	13.95	6.68	9.06	0.86	14.82	+/- S&P 500
-14.94	-10.91	14.05	-4.28	7.14	5.60	15.51	-7.66	2.62	12.34	8.64	22.33	+/- Wilshire SV
4.53	3.07	2.39	2.23	1.85	1.53	1.47	0.44	0.28	0.21	0.64	1.29	Income Return %
24.43	9.49	8.57	15.89	23.40	-15.33	63.04	21.13	16.46	10.16	37.76	36.47	Capital Return %
41		30	1	88	10	1	24	2	26	1	1	Total Rtn % Rank Cat
0.35	0.37	0.30	0.26	0.22	0.21	0.15	0.07	0.05	0.04	0.14	0.34	Income $
0.00	1.47	0.31	1.03	1.21	1.06	0.58	1.34	1.70	1.34	0.73	2.60	Capital Gains $
0.99	0.95	0.89	0.89	0.92	1.17	1.21	1.08	1.06	1.03	0.95	0.87	Expense Ratio %
3.90	3.38	2.55	1.66	1.77	1.37	1.32	0.55	0.29	0.20	0.48	1.28	Income Ratio %
76	34	44	31	22	21	12	13	19	16	11	21	Turnover Rate %
39.8	47.9	51.1	62.4	76.0	66.1	98.9	125.1	153.7	191.8	353.0	492.9	Net Assets $mil

Portfolio Manager(s)

Robert L. Rodriguez, CFA. Since 7-84. BS'71/ MBA'75 USC. Currently chief investment officer of First Pacific Advisors, Rodriguez joined the firm in 1983. Previously, he was a senior portfolio manager with Kaufman & Broad from 1981 to 1983, and spent the prior 10 years with Transamerica Investment Research. He was Morningstar Mutual Funds' Manager of the Year for 1994. He also manages FPA New Income.

Performance 12-31-96

	1st Qtr	2nd Qtr	3rd Qtr	4th Qtr	Total
1992	11.43	-11.68	0.84	22.50	21.57
1993	4.69	0.26	7.72	3.24	16.74
1994	1.45	-2.28	6.41	4.62	10.37
1995	10.09	16.12	12.28	-3.58	38.39
1996	8.85	8.02	5.96	10.57	37.76

Trailing	Total Return%	+/- S&P 500	+/- Wil Small Value	%Rank All	Cat	Growth of $10,000
3 Mo	10.57	2.24	2.28	4	16	11,057
6 Mo	17.16	5.48	6.89	3	3	11,716
1 Yr	37.76	14.82	22.33	2	4	13,776
3 Yr Avg	28.15	8.49	14.49	1	1	21,043
5 Yr Avg	24.46	9.26	7.75	1	1	29,866
10 Yr Avg	21.40	6.12	7.60	1	1	69,531
15 Yr Avg	18.57	1.79	-1.36	2	1	128,786

Tax Analysis	Tax-Adj Return %	% Pretax Return
3 Yr Avg	25.54	90.7
5 Yr Avg	21.70	88.7
10 Yr Avg	18.46	86.3

Potential Capital Gain Exposure: 38% of assets

Risk Analysis

Time Period	Load-Adj Return %	Risk %Rank All Cat	Morningstar Return	Morningstar Risk	Morningstar Risk-Adj Rating
1 Yr	28.81				
3 Yr	25.31	79 73	2.55	1.01	★★★★★
5 Yr	22.80	85 88	2.54	1.16	★★★★★
10 Yr	20.59	91 92	2.80	1.32	★★★★★

Average Historical Rating (133 months): 3.2★s

†1=low, 100=high

Category Rating (3 Yr)		Other Measures	Standard Index S&P 500	Best Fit Index SPMid400
		Alpha	8.4	11.9
Worst ... Best		Beta	1.00	1.04
		R-Squared	54	72
Return	High	Standard Deviation		16.38
Risk	Above Avg	Mean		25.88
		Sharpe Ratio		1.59

Analysis by Laura Lallos 01-17-97

FPA Capital Fund shows you don't have to be a bull to lead a bull run.

On the face of it, this fund didn't have the prescription for success in 1996. While it does have a big technology stake, it doesn't hold the Nasdaq bellwethers such as Intel that led the charge. Further, its cash stake has been higher than it has been in years, generally more than 20% of assets. Yet, not only did the fund lead the small-cap value category by a mile last year, but it lapped the formidable S&P 500.

As always, the fund's secret was a few great stocks. The fund has been in the right places lately, tech, retail, and financials, but these concentrations aren't the result of following the fads, as the fund's low turnover shows. Manager Bob Rodriguez's contrarian style leads him to buy a stock when it is out of favor and quite cheap relative to book value and earnings. The fund enjoyed triple-digit returns from several of its sizable top holdings in 1996—Ross Stores, Storage Technology,

and Coachmen Industries—yet still falls solidly in the value camp.

This great performance hasn't assuaged Rodriguez's concerns about a high-flying market. Granted, he found some bargains during 1996, including a typically unglamorous pick, CPI, the Sears photography studio, which is buying back its own shares. But the September shareholder report barely touched on the fund's outstanding returns, while dwelling on reasons why the rally can't continue. If things do indeed take a turn for the worse, though, this may be one of the best places to be. Although the fund suffered along with other small-cap value offerings in 1990's recession, double-digit returns in years such as 1987 and 1994 have contributed to this fund's long-term reign as one of the best in the business.

Results like that must be maddening for competitors—and investors who didn't get in before the fund closed.

Portfolio Analysis 09-30-96

Share Chg 06-96 000	Amount 000	Total Stocks: 33 Total Fixed-Income: 5	Value $000	% Net Assets
-4	1,025	Green Tree Financial	40,231	8.16
0	760	Ross Stores	27,353	5.55
20	435	Seagate Technology	24,306	4.93
1,000	1,000	Mac Frugals Bargains Close	23,625	4.79
0	565	Reebok International	19,634	3.98
0	500	Storage Technology	18,938	3.84
25	395	Arrow Electronics	17,586	3.57
308	681	Coachmen Industries	17,538	3.56
0	575	Comdisco	16,603	3.37
110	510	Marshall Industries	15,364	3.12
0	550	Countrywide Credit Industry	14,094	2.86
0	498	Quick & Reilly Group	13,075	2.65
0	10,000	Trump Atlantic City Fdg 11.25%	9,800	1.99
0	400	Angelica	8,650	1.75
10	500	Recoton	7,438	1.51
0	7,000	FNMA CMO PAC 8.5%	7,031	1.43
0	328	Komag	6,884	1.40
0	385	Quantum	6,762	1.37
17	357	CPI	6,699	1.36
0	200	Horace Mann Educators	6,575	1.33
0	275	Thor Industries	6,566	1.33
0	294	Westcorp	6,358	1.29
60	420	Exabyte	6,300	1.28
0	275	Rouge Steel Cl A	5,981	1.21
0	160	Fluke	5,896	1.20

Current Investment Style

Style		Stock Port Avg	Relative S&P 500 Current	Hist	Rel Cat
Value Blnd Growth	Large Med Small				
	Price/Earnings Ratio	17.9	0.75	0.8	0.88
	Price/Book Ratio	2.9	0.58	0.5	1.10
	5 Yr Earnings Gr%	20.6	1.18	2.0	1.32
	Price/Cash Flow	10.4	0.76	1.0	0.89
	Debt % Total Cap	21.8	0.70	0.7	0.72
	Med Mkt Cap $mil	1,238	0.1	0.1	2.31
	Foreign %	0.0	—	—	0.00

†figure is based on 50% or less of stocks

Special Securities	% of assets 09-30-96
○ Private/Illiquid Securities	0
○ Emerging-Markets Secs	0
○ Options/Futures/Warrants	No

Composition	% of assets 09-30-96		Market Cap	
		Giant	0.0	
Cash	22.4	Large	18.3	
Stocks	71.2	Medium	36.2	
Bonds	5.9	Small	30.0	
Other	0.5	Micro	15.6	

Sector Weightings	% of Stocks	Rel S&P	5-Year High	Low
Utilities	0.0	0.0	0	0
Energy	0.0	0.0	0	0
Financials	23.5	1.7	33	13
Ind Cycls	11.0	0.7	21	11
Cons Dur	13.8	3.5	19	0
Cons Stpls	0.0	0.0	0	0
Services	9.9	0.8	11	0
Retail	16.3	3.2	17	0
Health	0.0	0.0	14	0
Tech	25.6	2.1	33	18

Address:	11400 W. Olympic Boulevard Suite 1200 Los Angeles, CA 90064 800-982-4372 / 310-473-0225	Minimum Purchase:	Closed	Add: $100	IRA: —
		Min Auto Inv Plan:	Closed	Systematic Inv: $100	
		Date of Inception:	02-01-68		
Advisor:	First Pacific Advisors	Sales Fees:	6.50%L		
Subadvisor:	None	Management Fee:	0.75% max./0.65% min., 0.10%A		
Distributor:	FPA Fund Distributors	Actual Fees:	Mgt: 0.65%	Dist: —	
States Available:	All plus PR	Expense Projections:	5Yr: $91	5Yr: $110	10Yr: $165
Report Grade:	B+	Annual Brokerage Cost:	0.04%	Income Distrib: Semi-Ann.	
NTF Plans:	N/A	**Total Cost** (relative to category):	Below Avg		

© 1997 Morningstar, Inc. All rights reserved. 225 W. Wacker Dr., Chicago, IL 60606, 312-696-6000
Although data are gathered from reliable sources, Morningstar cannot guarantee completeness and accuracy.

MORNINGSTAR   Mutual Funds

Source: Morningstar Mutual Funds. Reprinted by permission.

ALL IN THE (FUND) FAMILY

One of the best places to find mutual fund information is online. Most, if not all fund families, have web sites that allow users to read about a family's various fund options and get applications. Among some of popular fund families are:

AIM
800-347-4246
http://www.aimfunds.com

American Century Investments
800-345-2021
http://www.americancentury.com

The Berger Funds
800-333-1001
http://www.bergerfunds.com

Fidelity Investments
800-544-8888
http://www.fid-inv.com/

INVESCO
800-525-8085
http://www.invesco.com

Janus Funds
800-525-3713
http://www.janusfunds.com

Scudder
800-225-2470
http://www.scudder.com

Strong Funds
800-368-1030
http://www.strong-funds.com

T. Rowe Price
800-638-5660
http://www.troweprice.com

The Vanguard Group
800-662-7447
http://www.vanguard.com

What's often a choice, although not always clearly enumerated for a number of funds, is the automatic monthly deposit option. As noted earlier, this set-up means that the mutual fund company will automatically deduct a certain amount from your checking account each month, often only $50. But more important, by signing up for this service, and presumably making a long-term commitment to the company, the mutual fund will waive the minimum start-up cost. This isn't pure benevolence on their end: You are promising them a steady, albeit small, future cash flow. To find out which funds offer this and exactly what type of arrangements they offer, give them a call. Most funds have an 800 number listed in *Morningstar* and a number of other sources. Start cheap. One of the benefits of mutual funds is that many allow investors to start with just a few bucks, if they agree to regularly contribute to the fund every month. In the box are 10 no-load fund families, top-rated by *Morningstar*, that allow investors to open an account for just $50.

Dollar-Cost Averaging

Automatic monthly payments also provide another investing bonus, something called dollar-cost averaging. Dollar-cost averaging is simply making equal payments into an investment, like a mutual fund, at regular intervals, such as every month. Since you're always investing the same amount of money, you'll naturally buy more shares when the price drops and less when it goes up. Over time, this has the effect of lowering your overall cost. As the table shows, even though New Vision's NAV remained at $10 after five months, the portfolio had still gained in value by $44.60. Sure, that doesn't sound like much, but remember, this is only for a few months, and it sure beats just breaking even.

START CHEAP . . .

One of the benefits of mutual funds is that many allow investors to start with just a few bucks, if they agree to regularly contribute to the fund every month. Below are 10 no-load fund families, top-rated by *Morningstar*, that allow investors to open an account for just $50.

Name	**Phone**
Smith Breeden	800-221-3138
American Century	800-331-8331
Preferred	800-662-4769
Strong Funds	800-368-1030
T. Rowe Price	800-638-5660
Fremont	800-548-4539
Marshall Equity-Income	800-236-8560
INVESCO	800-525-8085
Columbia	800-547-1707
Homestead	800-258-3030

Source: Morningstar Mutual Funds

Taking the Plunge: Buying a Mutual Fund

Well, it's show time! After selecting the fund or funds you may be interested in, the next step is to obtain information directly from the fund, including the prospectus and the application for purchasing a fund. To get this information, just about all mutual fund companies have toll-free phone numbers; and most have web sites that allow you to sign up for free material. Incidentally, don't be concerned when you call and they say the "conversation is being taped on a recorded line." This is a formality mutual fund companies follow to protect themselves. And speaking of law, mutual fund companies cannot legally sell you a fund until you have read the prospectus.

DOLLAR-COST AVERAGING				
Purchasing Date	**Total Amount Invested**	**New Vision Mutual NAV**	**Shares Purchased**	**Total Portfolio Value**
January 1	$100.00	$10.00	10.00	$100.00
February 1	$100.00	$9.00	11.11	$189.99
March 1	$100.00	$8.50	11.76	$279.40
April 1	$100.00	$8.00	12.50	$362.96
May 1	$100.00	$11.00	9.09	$599.06
June 1	$100.00	$10.00	10.00	$644.60
Ending Values	**$600.00**	**$10.00**	**64.46**	**$644.60**

The mutual fund account application is usually a one or two page form asking basics like name, address, phone, employer, and so forth. In addition to these questions, the company will also ask you to select the fund in which you want to invest and how much you would like to start off with. In addition, if you opt for the automatic deposit system, they'll usually ask for a voided blank check to be attached to the application to convey the proper account information for the electronic monthly transfer.

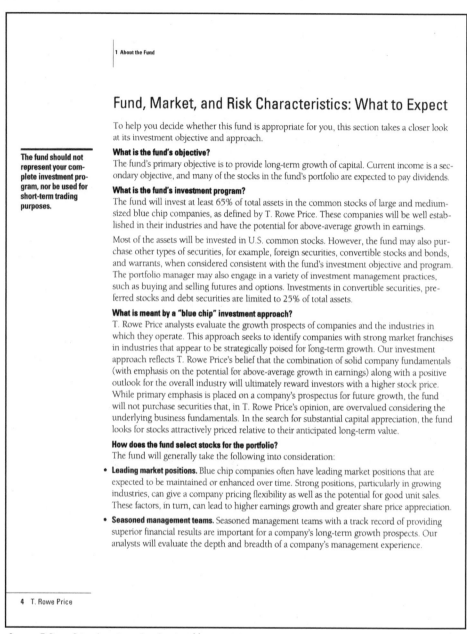

1 About the Fund

Fund, Market, and Risk Characteristics: What to Expect

To help you decide whether this fund is appropriate for you, this section takes a closer look at its investment objective and approach.

What is the fund's objective?

The fund's primary objective is to provide long-term growth of capital. Current income is a secondary objective, and many of the stocks in the fund's portfolio are expected to pay dividends.

What is the fund's investment program?

The fund will invest at least 65% of total assets in the common stocks of large and medium-sized blue chip companies, as defined by T. Rowe Price. These companies will be well established in their industries and have the potential for above-average growth in earnings.

Most of the assets will be invested in U.S. common stocks. However, the fund may also purchase other types of securities, for example, foreign securities, convertible stocks and bonds, and warrants, when considered consistent with the fund's investment objective and program. The portfolio manager may also engage in a variety of investment management practices, such as buying and selling futures and options. Investments in convertible securities, preferred stocks and debt securities are limited to 25% of total assets.

What is meant by a "blue chip" investment approach?

T. Rowe Price analysts evaluate the growth prospects of companies and the industries in which they operate. This approach seeks to identify companies with strong market franchises in industries that appear to be strategically poised for long-term growth. Our investment approach reflects T. Rowe Price's belief that the combination of solid company fundamentals (with emphasis on the potential for above-average growth in earnings) along with a positive outlook for the overall industry will ultimately reward investors with a higher stock price. While primary emphasis is placed on a company's prospectus for future growth, the fund will not purchase securities that, in T. Rowe Price's opinion, are overvalued considering the underlying business fundamentals. In the search for substantial capital appreciation, the fund looks for stocks attractively priced relative to their anticipated long-term value.

How does the fund select stocks for the portfolio?

The fund will generally take the following into consideration:

- **Leading market positions.** Blue chip companies often have leading market positions that are expected to be maintained or enhanced over time. Strong positions, particularly in growing industries, can give a company pricing flexibility as well as the potential for good unit sales. These factors, in turn, can lead to higher earnings growth and greater share price appreciation.

- **Seasoned management teams.** Seasoned management teams with a track record of providing superior financial results are important for a company's long-term growth prospects. Our analysts will evaluate the depth and breadth of a company's management experience.

The fund should not represent your complete investment program, nor be used for short-term trading purposes.

4   T. Rowe Price

Source: T. Rowe Price Associates, Inc. Reprinted by permission.

Aside from these standard questions, about the only potentially confusing section deals with capital gains and dividend distributions. Depending on what type of mutual fund you choose, there's a strong chance that the fund will issue capital gains or dividend payments to shareholders periodically, generally four times a year. Capital gains payments are when the

Prospectus: *The document that describes a mutual fund's investment objectives, policies, fees, etc. By law, it must be furnished to all investors.*

mutual fund manager buys a stock at, say, $20 a share and sells it at a later date for a profit, let's say $30 a share. That $10 profit, known as a capital gain, is passed onto shareholders. Distributions are made either at the end of the year or in quarterly payouts. Also, if a stock or bond owned by the fund pays out a dividend or interest, that money goes to the mutual fund, which in turn passes it along to shareholders. These payments can be distributed with or separately from capital gains distributions.

Capital gains and dividend distributions are passed along to the shareholder as a per share amount. For example, suppose the mutual fund earned $2 million in capital gains when the fund manager sold a stock that increased in value. The mutual fund, which had 10 million outstanding shares, would pay out that capital gain in the form of $.20 per share. So if as a shareholder you owned 70 shares, you'd receive $14 in capital gains distributions (70 x $.20=$14). The process happens with dividends as well. The difference with dividends, however, is that the stock was not sold by the fund manager. The company simply paid a quarterly profit out to it's shareholders, which in this case included the mutual fund.

When purchasing a mutual fund, investors are given two options in how they would like to receive these capital gains and dividend distributions. They can either receive them in cash, as a check cut by the mutual fund company and mailed to them when they are

announced, or they can elect to have the money reinvested into the mutual fund for purchasing additional shares. For example, suppose the New Vision fund, with a current NAV of $10, announces capital gains and dividends one quarter totaling $.25 per share. If you owned 50 shares, you could receive either $12.50 in cash (50 x $25 = $12.50) or have it reinvested into the fund to buy more shares, in this case 1.25 more shares. Finance experts usually suggest having these payments reinvested, as they help compound the growth of the investment. Regardless of which option you choose, it's extremely important to remember this: Whether you receive these payments in cash or have them reinvested, you are liable for taxes on them in the year they were paid out. In other words, if the New Vision fund paid out $.25 a share in capital gains and dividends, and you received $12.50 total, you would be required to pay taxes on that amount *even if this was reinvested to purchase more shares and you never actually took*

home, or realized, the payment. Your mutual fund company will send you a tax form called a 1099-DIV at the beginning of the year which will show exactly what capital gains you earned throughout the year and what you will then owe taxes on.

Tracking Your Fund

One of the cool things about owning a mutual fund is that you can track it's worth in the newspaper every day, (or if you're wired online). Like stocks, mutual funds are usually listed in the business section of the newspaper, alphabetically by fund family: Scudder, T. Rowe Price, Putnam, etc. Under each family name, the funds of that family are listed alphabetically if there is more than one. Although newspapers vary in how they list their data, most usually show the following information listed in the sample table on page 98. In addition to tracking a fund in the paper or online, the mutual fund company will also issue periodic statements about the fund, often written by the fund manager. These statements, while they're normally filled with the somewhat self-serving jargon that fills most semipromotional material, also contain some interesting data about the fund. For example, the annual or quarterly statements often list the top 10 holdings–stocks, bonds, or other securities by total dollar worth–of the fund and give some insight to what the fund manager hopes to accomplish in the particular market environment.

> **This will not be on the test.** Martini anyone? From 1995 to 1996, the number of premium cigars imported into the United States jumped 67 percent, from 164 to 274 million units. Overall, the total consumption of all large cigars stood at 3 billion units for 1996. However, that's just one-third the 9 billion smokers chomped on in 1964.
>
> Source: Cigar Association of America

If you sign up for the automatic monthly deposit program, you may receive a monthly statement confirming your purchase, including how many shares were purchased, at what price, and any

MUTUAL FUND QUOTATIONS

Name	NAV	Net Chg	YTD %ret
A Mgr	18.20	+0.03	+12.3
AMgrGr	18.85	+0.04	+15.3
Balanc	15.64	...	+13.3
BluCh	38.58	+0.09	+18.0
CAInsM	10.47	−0.01	+ 3.7
CAMun	11.94	−0.01	+ 3.8
Canad r	19.00	+0.05	+ 7.8
CapAp	20.35	+0.04	+15.4
CpInc r	9.68	...	+ 6.0
CngS	298.37	−0.93	+19.2
Contra	46.01	+0.12	+11.0
CnvSc	18.50	+0.09	+ 7.7
DestI	23.51	+0.07	+17.4
DestII	13.54	+0.04	+16.6
DisEq	25.95	+0.07	+17.7
DivIntl	16.68	−0.01	+13.4
DivGth	23.23	+0.03	+15.6
EmGr r	27.40	+0.22	+ 8.8
EmrMkt r	16.14	−0.06	− 2.9
Eq Inc	49.48	...	+18.1
EQII	27.43	−0.01	+17.2
Europ r	29.64	−0.19	+11.4
ErCapAp r	15.60	−0.04	+14.8
Exch	192.74	−0.23	+21.7
Export	18.37	+0.11	+ 9.7
Fidel	28.96	+0.05	+17.9
Fifty	16.21	+0.04	+15.5
GNMA	10.73	−0.02	+ 3.4
GloBal	14.74	...	+10.3
GloBd	9.32	...	− 1.6
GovtSc	9.64	−0.01	+ 2.5
GroCo	45.99	+0.11	+13.9
GroInc	36.10	+0.01	+18.2
HKChna	15.05	−0.10	+ 5.9
IntBd	10.05	−0.01	+ 2.7
IntGr	21.26	−0.05	+ 8.7
IntVal	13.11	−0.04	+13.5
InvGB	7.11	−0.01	+ 2.8
Japan r	13.18	−0.01	+15.4
JpnSmCo r	8.39	+0.03	+ 5.7
LargeCap	13.79	+0.04	+14.5
LatinAm r	17.86	+0.12	+36.2
LmtMun	9.76	...	+ 3.2
LowP r	23.55	+0.04	+10.3
MagIn	91.56	+0.12	+16.5
MidCap	15.43	+0.08	+10.5
MtgSec	10.93	−0.01	+ 3.7
MunBd	8.29	...	+ 3.5
MuniInc	12.41	−0.01	+ 3.5
NewMkt r	14.29	−0.07	+13.6
NewMill	23.12	+0.29	+14.4
Nordic	15.00	−0.01	+ 8.7
NYMun	12.51	−0.01	+ 3.9
NYInsM	11.82	...	+ 3.2
OTC	34.81	+0.38	+ 6.4
Ovrse	35.27	−0.09	+14.4
PcBas r	16.18	...	+10.1
Puritn	19.42	−0.03	+14.6
RealE	18.43	−0.10	+ 4.2
RetGr	19.60	+0.02	+13.4
SIntGv	9.32	−0.01	+ 2.3
STBF	8.69	...	+ 2.6
SmallCap	14.54	+0.04	+ 9.5
SE Asia r	14.51	−0.04	− 3.5
StrOpp	24.49	−0.01	+11.0
StkSlc	27.69	+0.04	+16.1
TechqGr	11.19	+0.09	+ 8.3
Trend	60.46	+0.57	+ 6.9
USBI	10.53	−0.01	+ 3.0
Utility	18.09	−0.02	+ 9.4
Value	59.52	+0.14	+15.5
Wrldw	17.38	...	+12.9
Fidelity Selects:			
Air r	21.42	−0.10	+10.4
AmGold r	21.48	−0.17	−12.8
Auto r	26.07	−0.04	+10.3
Biotech r	33.27	−0.14	+ 4.4
Broker r	29.23	+0.02	+26.4
Chem r	46.16	+0.06	+11.3
Comp r	47.08	+1.28	+ 5.2
CstHou r	21.92	−0.07	+15.8
ConInd r	22.67	−0.01	+15.5
GrwthA p	34.87	+0.30	+ 7.4
GrwthB t	34.19	+0.30	+ 7.1
GrwthH t	34.20	+0.30	+ 7.1
GrwthZ	35.00	+0.31	+ 7.6
GrIncA p	12.95	+0.01	+12.4
HiYldA p	7.67	...	+ 4.3
HiYldB t	7.67	...	+ 4.0
HiYldH t	7.66	−0.01	+ 3.9
TF MNE	10.40	−0.01	+ 3.0
TF NatE	10.96	−0.01	+ 3.3
USGvtA p	9.01	−0.02	+ 2.8
USGvtE	9.01	−0.01	+ 2.9
USGvtH t	8.99	−0.01	+ 2.4
ValuA p	13.40	−0.05	+14.4
Forum Funds:			
InvBnd	10.27	−0.01	+ 3.5
ME Bnd	10.90	...	+ 2.9
Tax Svr	10.64	...	+ 2.8
Founders Funds:			
Bal p	11.72	−0.01	+11.0
BlueC p	8.21	...	+13.6
Discv p	23.91	+0.17	− 1.3
Frntr p	32.31	+0.05	− 0.1
GovSc	9.03	−0.01	+ 2.2
Gwth p	18.63	+0.11	+17.4
IntlEq p	13.56	−0.01	+14.3
Passprt	14.97	−0.03	+ 7.6
Specl p	8.41	+0.03	+ 9.8
WldGr p	24.09	+0.01	+10.6
Fountain Square Fds:			
Balanced	14.54	+0.05	+14.7
BondIncA	12.08	...	NS
EqIncA	13.88	+0.03	NS
GovtSec	9.67	...	+ 2.5
IntEq	11.64	−0.08	+11.4
MidCap	15.48	+0.09	+11.8
MuniBdA	12.19	−0.01	NS
OhioTF	10.20	−0.01	+ 2.7
QualBd	9.70	−0.01	+ 2.5
QualGr	18.16	+0.09	+22.7
Franklin Class I:			
AGE I p	2.93	...	+ 5.4
AdjUS p	9.43	+0.01	+ 3.6
AL TF I p	11.80	...	+ 3.4
AZInTFI p	10.48	−0.01	+ 3.7
AZ TF I p	11.30	...	+ 3.2
AstAlc p	9.16	−0.02	+10.6
BalInv p	32.06	+0.03	+13.3
CA Gro I	21.37	+0.09	+ 4.9
CAHYBd p	10.23	...	+ 4.1
CalInsI p	12.31	−0.01	+ 3.1
CA Intl p	10.97	−0.01	+ 3.3
CalTF I p	7.21	...	+ 3.2
CO TF I p	11.86	−0.01	+ 3.2
CpQuI p	23.95	+0.01	+ 3.3
CT TF I p	10.98	...	+ 3.3
CvtScI p	13.82	+0.04	+ 8.8
DynatI p	16.95	+0.12	+11.4
EquityI p	10.20	+0.01	+17.3
EqInI p	18.59	...	+12.8
FedInt p	10.97	−0.01	+ 2.8
FedTxI	12.08	...	+ 3.6
FIST ARS p	9.95	...	+ 3.6
FL TF I p	11.65	...	+ 3.3
FLTFIn p	10.10	...	+ 3.5
GA TF I p	11.91	...	+ 3.0
GlGvInI p	8.46	...	− 0.1
GlHlthI p	18.83	−0.11	+ 5.4
GlUtil I p	15.93	+0.11	+13.6
GoldI p	12.13	−0.11	− 8.2
GrwthI p	26.20	+0.02	+11.8
HIMun I p	10.91	...	+ 3.1
HY TF I p	11.28	...	+ 3.9
IncomI p	2.41	...	+ 6.1
IN TFI p	11.83	...	+ 3.2
InsTF I p	12.20	−0.01	+ 3.0
InvGd p	9.02	...	+ 2.0
KYTF I p	11.12	−0.01	+ 3.3
LA TF I p	11.37	...	+ 3.2
MD TF I p	11.39	...	+ 3.3
MA TF I p	11.63	−0.01	+ 3.5
MicVal I p	20.40	+0.02	+ 8.8
SmCapG	21.84	+0.05	+17.9
Value p	13.72	...	+19.1
Galaxy Funds Retail:			
AstAll p	15.78	...	+11.1
CT Mu p	10.32	...	+ 3.2
EqGth p	23.31	+0.04	+16.5
EqIncm p	18.43	−0.08	+15.3
EqtVal p	17.11	...	+16.4
GrInEq p	15.64	+0.03	+17.6
HiQ Bd p	10.43	−0.02	+ 2.6
IntGvBd p	10.04	−0.01	+ 2.9
IntlEq p	15.76	−0.08	+15.0
LargeCo	27.37	+0.01	+21.5
MA Mu p	10.11	−0.01	+ 3.4
MuniBd	10.34	...	+ 2.8
NY Mu p	10.93	−0.01	+ 3.2
ST Bd p	9.96	...	+ 2.4
SmCpVl p	15.27	+0.02	+10.5
SmCoEq p	18.35	+0.09	+ 3.3
SmallCo	25.46	+0.09	+ 8.9
TE Bond p	10.94	−0.01	+ 3.3
USTreas	10.19	−0.02	+ 2.5
Utility	12.13	+0.03	+ 5.0
Galaxy Funds Trust:			
AstAl	15.78	−0.01	+11.1
EqGro	23.33	+0.05	+16.7
EqInc	18.43	−0.08	+15.5
EqVal	17.10	...	+16.6
GrInEq	15.66	+0.03	+17.8
HiQBd	10.43	−0.02	+ 2.7
IntGvBd	10.04	−0.01	+ 3.0
IntCorBd	10.44	−0.02	+ 2.6
IntlEq	15.89	−0.08	+15.3
NYMuni	10.93	−0.01	+ 3.3
SmCoEq	18.66	+0.09	+ 3.4
SmCpVl	15.31	+0.02	+10.6
ShtTm	9.96	...	+ 2.4
TxEBd	10.94	−0.01	+ 3.4
Gateway:			
CIntl	16.97	+0.04	+10.2
IndxPl	19.42	+0.04	+ 5.4
SmCap	13.10	+0.04	+ 8.6
GenSec	18.28	...	+13.5
Gintel Group:			
Gintel	20.24	+0.40	+11.8
Glenmede Funds:			
EmgMkts	11.80	+0.01	+19.2
Equity	20.69	+0.04	+17.3
IntGov	10.21	−0.01	+ 3.1
IntIntl	15.98	−0.04	+ 9.4
IntlPt	16.32	−0.03	+10.0
LrgCapV	14.96	+0.04	+20.0
MunInt	10.31	...	+ 2.8
SmCap	20.20	+0.03	+14.0
GoldenOk DG p	13.62	+0.19	+13.0
GoldenOk IB	9.83	−0.01	+ 2.4
Goldman Sachs Funds:			
AdjRtGvA	9.89	...	+ 3.2
AsiaGrA	16.08	+0.02	− 1.2
BalanceA	20.44	+0.06	+12.6
CapGrA	19.17	−0.01	+22.1
CoreEqA	26.56	+0.04	+20.7
GlbIncA	14.72	−0.02	+ 2.8
GovIncA p	14.26	−0.02	+ 3.0
GrIncA	26.75	+0.17	+20.4
IntlEqA	22.09	−0.01	+10.8
MunIncA	14.74	−0.01	+ 4.0
SmCapA	23.85	+0.23	+15.9
GvtBond	20.85	−0.01	+ 2.9
GvtEqty	38.21	+0.02	+19.1
Govett Funds:			
EmgMkts	15.44	+0.01	+13.0
GlobInc	7.77	−0.01	− 3.9
IntlEq	12.15	−0.05	+ 8.6
PfcStg	9.81	+0.01	+ 7.3
SmCos	19.17	+0.15	−12.2
Gradison Funds:			
EstVal p	31.19	−0.02	+14.6
GovInc p	12.91	−0.02	+ 3.1
GrInc p	24.29	+0.04	+18.2
Intl p	17.82	−0.09	+11.1
OH TF p	13.45	−0.01	+ 3.7
IndInc p	15.44	...	+15.4
IntGov	12.42	−0.01	+ 2.1
IntlGr	18.37	−0.05	+10.5
Ltn Amer Gr p	17.38	+0.18	+31.1
Leisur	25.16	−0.03	+11.4
MulAstAl p	13.17	...	+ 9.6
PcBas	13.99	−0.01	+ 2.9
Realty	10.23	−0.05	NS
SelInc p	6.61	−0.01	+ 4.2
ShTrBd p	9.50	...	+ 2.6
SmCoGth p	13.15	+0.07	+ 5.0
SmCoVal	13.91	+0.01	+12.0
TxFre p	15.43	−0.01	+ 3.6
Tech	33.44	+0.40	+ 7.9
TotRtn	27.45	+0.02	+14.2
USGvt p	7.42	−0.02	+ 2.8
Util	11.99	+0.05	+ 6.6
ValEq	28.13	+0.07	+18.8
WldCap p	11.97	...	+24.8
WldCom p	14.29	+0.08	+13.1
INVESCO Advisor:			
EquityC p	97.75	+0.19	+18.8
FlexC p	75.45	...	+13.9
IncomeC p	48.84	−0.04	+ 2.3
IntlValC p	60.22	−0.25	+12.2
MultiFlxC p	57.54	−0.05	+ 9.7
RealEstC	57.50	−0.16	+ 1.6
ISI Funds:			
Muni p	10.67	...	+ 3.3
NoAm p	8.47	−0.01	+ 3.2
Trst p	9.70	−0.02	+ 2.1
Independence One:			
EqPlus	15.59	+0.01	+21.4
FixInc	9.89	−0.01	+ 2.5
MIMuBd	10.23	−0.01	+ 3.2
USGvTr	10.10	−0.01	+ 2.5
Integrity Mutual Fds:			
FdFnds fr	13.53	+0.01	+ 8.0
KS InsI	12.28	...	+ 2.3
KS Mun	12.39	−0.01	+ 3.5
MT TxFr	10.17	−0.01	+ 3.3
ND TxFr r	9.27	−0.03	+ 3.3
NE Mun	11.21	−0.01	+ 3.3
Inv Resh	4.43	...	+13.6
Investors Trust:			
GovA p	8.44	...	+ 3.2
GovB t	8.45	...	+ 2.9
GroB	15.13	+0.08	+15.0
ValB	12.91	+0.03	+24.1
Ivy Funds:			
Bond p	10.03	−0.01	+ 5.4
Canada p	9.16	−0.04	− 5.0
ChinaA p	11.31	+0.04	+ 9.8
ChinaB p	11.25	+0.04	+ 9.4
EmGrA p	25.54	+0.20	− 3.8
EmGrB r	25.27	+0.20	− 4.0
Global p	14.67	−0.03	+11.4
GrthA p	19.32	+0.06	+ 8.8
GrInA p	12.81	+0.04	+12.9
GrIncB p	12.75	+0.04	+12.6
IntlA p	40.48	−0.22	+12.8
IntlB p	40.15	−0.21	+12.4
IntlC	39.98	−0.22	+12.4
IntlI	40.56	−0.22	NA
NewCntA p	11.41	...	+12.7
JPM Pierpont Funds:			
Bond	10.25	−0.01	+ 3.4
Divrf	13.93	...	+12.0
EmgMEq	12.18	+0.03	+18.0
Equity	25.72	+0.01	+19.1
IntlEq	11.92	−0.05	+ 9.1
IntlOpp	10.76	−0.03	NS
NYToRBd	10.52	−0.01	+ 2.9
SmCo	26.86	+0.10	+ 7.5
TEBond	11.85	−0.01	+ 3.0
JPM Instl Funds:			
Bond	9.85	−0.01	+ 3.5
DiscEq	12.10	+0.01	NS
Diversifd	13.43	...	+12.1
EmgMkEq	12.27	+0.03	+18.1
Equity	16.35	...	+19.2
IntlEqty	12.37	−0.04	+ 9.3
IndxEq	17.75	+0.01	+21.3
IntlGr	16.06	−0.12	+ 9.3
SmCoGro	17.25	+0.02	+13.4
Key Funds:			
SBSF Conv	13.72	−0.01	+ 7.7
SBSF Fnd	17.54	−0.03	+ 6.0
SBSFCapG	9.90	+0.04	− 1.3
StkIdx	13.00	...	+20.9
KeyPremier Funds:			
AggGrwthR	10.35	+0.14	NS
EstGrwthR	11.24	+0.03	+15.0
IntTmIncR	9.84	−0.01	+ 2.3
PA MuBd	10.35	...	+ 1.9
Keystone:			
QultyB1 t	15.15	−0.02	+ 2.3
DivrB2 t	15.33	−0.02	+ 3.6
HiIncB4 t	4.30	...	+ 4.8
BalK1 t	13.04	−0.03	+11.6
StrGrK2 t	9.52	+0.02	+17.8
GrIncS1 t	29.31	+0.03	+16.7
MidCapS3 t	9.10	+0.03	+ 4.7
SmCoGrS4 t	8.68	+0.05	+ 3.1
Intl t	9.24	−0.01	+13.4
PrecMtl t	19.70	−0.21	−11.5
TaxF t	7.76	...	+ 3.1
Keystone America A:			
CapPreA	9.81	...	+ 3.3
FLTxFA	10.65	−0.01	+ 2.5
FndAmA	15.60	+0.12	+35.4
GloOpA	23.19	+0.09	+ 0.7
GvSecA	9.62	−0.01	+ 3.1
HrtEmGrA	27.86	+0.37	+ 4.9
IntmBdA	8.96	−0.02	+ 2.9
MOTxFA	9.94	−0.01	+ 4.0
OmegA	20.17	+0.05	+ 8.0
PaTxFA	11.43	−0.01	+ 3.7
SmCoGr2A p	10.71	+0.04	+ 2.8
GloResA	13.26	+0.01	+12.8
StrIncA	7.00	−0.01	+ 2.8
TaxFA	9.92	−0.01	+ 3.5
TotRtA	19.56	+0.03	+13.8
WldBdA	8.95	...	+ 1.5
Keystone America B:			
CAITxFB	9.70	−0.01	+ 3.4
CapPreB t	9.82	...	+ 2.9
FLTxFB t	10.53	...	+ 2.3
FndAmB t	15.36	+0.12	+35.0
GloOpB t	22.43	+0.09	+ 0.3
GvSecB t	9.62	−0.01	+ 2.8
IntmBdB t	8.98	−0.01	+ 2.7
MATxFB	9.43	−0.01	+ 3.7
MOTxFB	9.82	−0.01	+ 3.7
NYITxFB	9.83	−0.01	+ 3.2
OmegaB t	19.34	+0.04	+ 7.5
PaTxFB t	11.28	−0.01	+ 3.2
SmCGr2B p	10.59	+0.04	+ 2.4
GloResB t	13.00	+0.01	+12.4
StrIncB t	7.03	−0.01	+ 2.3
TaxFB t	9.83	−0.01	+ 3.2
TotRtB	19.53	+0.03	+13.4
Keystone America C:			
FLTxFC t	10.55	...	+ 2.3
FndAmC t	15.36	+0.12	+35.0
GloOpC t	22.47	+0.09	+ 0.3
GvSecC t	9.63	−0.01	+ 2.8
InstAdj Z	9.75	...	+ 3.4
IntmBdC t	8.97	−0.02	+ 2.6
MOTxFC	9.82	...	+ 3.7
OmegaC t	19.38	+0.05	+ 7.5
PaTxFC t	11.32	...	+ 3.3
SmCGr2C p	10.59	+0.04	+ 2.4
GloResC t	13.00	+0.01	+12.4
StrIncC t	7.02	−0.01	+ 2.3
TaxFC t	9.83	−0.01	+ 3.1
TotRtC	19.55	+0.04	+13.4
Kiewit Funds:			
Eqty	20.60	+0.03	+15.4
IntTmBd	2.04	...	+ 2.9
ShTmGov	2.01	...	+ 2.7
TxE	2.05	−0.01	+ 2.5
KobrenGrow t	11.54	+0.03	+12.7
LKCM Eq	12.91	+0.03	+16.1

dividends or capital gains that were declared by the firm. This is helpful for tax purposes and keeping close tabs on where the investment currently stands.

Selling a Fund

Summer comes and you decide to finally buy a new car and put the current rust bucket to pasture. You decide to cash in your mutual fund to cover the down payment. Here's how it works. When you decide to sell all or some of your mutual fund shares, you can call or write (currently, most funds will not allow you to do this via e-mail, however, some let you do it over the phone) with your request. The fund representative, for security reasons, will generally verify some data,

like Social Security number or mother's maiden name, to verify the legitimacy of the request. Once cleared, the fund will either send you a check for the appropriate amount or transfer it electronically to your savings or checking account, depending on which you specify. This may take a couple of days to a week, depending on the fund.

Mutual funds companies will cash you out at the price of the fund at the close of business on the day the order to sell is received. In other words, if a fund is selling for $15.50 during the day, the price you will receive per share would be $15.50.

When a mutual fund is sold, the Internal Revenue Service takes a particular interest in your action because there is usually a tax issue. In general, you'll either owe money if you made a profit or you can take a deduction (called a capital loss) if you lost money. There are a number of complicated rules that accompany the selling of securities, including mutual funds. It's not a bad idea to consult with the IRS or an accountant.

Q.u.i.c.k. D.o.w.n.l.o.a.d.

- Mutual funds are investment companies that pool the money of many individuals and invest it into stocks, bonds, and other securities under the guidance of a professional manager.

- The share price of a mutual fund, known as the net asset value, or NAV, is determined by taking the total assets of the fund, minus expenses, and dividing by the number of shares outstanding. NAVs rise and fall, based upon the value of the fund's holdings, not by the number of investors who purchase shares of the fund. This is different from stock prices, which move up or down based upon buyer and seller demands.

- Mutual funds make money for their investors in a few different ways. The first is when the holdings of the fund itself increase in value and are sold for a profit, known as capital gain. That income is passed onto the investor in the form of a "distribution." The second way a fund makes money for its investors is when the stock, bonds or other assets held by the fund produce income either as the result of dividends (from stocks) or interest (from bonds). These distributions can either be recieved as cash or reinvested to purchase more shares of the fund. A final way that a shareholder can make money with a mutual fund is when the NAV (net asset value) increases, and the shares are sold off at the increased price.

- Mutual funds offer shareholders, especially those just staring out, a number of advantages over individual stocks. These advantages include diversification (spreading of risk over many stocks and bonds), professional management, ease of setup, and cost controls.

- Some mutual funds charge a fee, known as a load. Loads are measured in percentages ranging from 3 to 8 percent. Fees applied to the purchase of shares are known as front-end loads; those attached to selling shares are called back-end loads, or redemption fees. Funds that do not charge either fee are called no-load funds. Some funds also have a different charge called a 12b-1 fee. All funds, however, charge investors for management or administrative fees. This charge is taken from the total assets of the fund and is calculated differently from loads.

- The single best source of information on mutual funds is a publication called *Morningstar*. Available at most libraries, this publication gives tons of information—including past performance, risk, and objectives—on virtually all funds in which the average person might consider investing.

- Many mutual funds require investors to open an account with a minimum amount of $1000 to $2500. Some are as high as $100,000. However, many funds will waive the minimum deposit altogether if the investor agrees to sign up for an automatic monthly deposit. In this arrangement, the investor agrees to invest a set amount of money to the fund every month. This payment is done electronically from a checking account or paycheck.

- Before buying a fund, investors are required to read the company's literature, including a publication known as the prospectus. Although not great beach reading, the prospectus outlines all the information about the fund, including its objectives and what it costs to open.

- Once a fund is purchased, an investor can track the NAV daily in the business section of the local paper. The paper will usually list the NAV, its daily price change, the year-to-date return, and whether or not the fund has recently issued a dividend.

- To sell a fund, an investor will usually need to call the fund and request that some or all the shares be sold. Once this is done, the individual will usually receive a check for the appropriate amount, usually within a few days.

- Investors have to pay taxes on a mutual fund whenever they make a profit from it. One way this happens is when the fund issues a dividend or capital gain distribution to shareholders. Regardless of whether this distribution is received in the form of a check or reinvested to purchase more shares, the investor must declare that income for tax purposes in the year the payment was issued. Tax liabilities may also occur when an investor sells a fund at a price higher than what was paid for the shares purchased. This is known as a capital gain.

4 Grad School, Travel, or New Wheels: Saving for Short-Term Goals

You're only here once so you got to get it right.–XTC

Julie Gets Schooled

Say hello to Julie. She's here to keep you from making costly mistakes with your short-term savings. From the moment she finished college, Julie set her academic sights on an MBA–with the explicit goal of starting business school within three years. When she graduated from college, Julie landed a sales job at a pharmaceutical company, making a base salary of $25,000 plus sales commissions. At the end of her first year, between her base pay and commissions from sales, Julie pulled in a total of $30,000.

At the same time she started her job, Julie disciplined herself about saving for the short term, particularly business school tuition. Of the schools she considered applying to, the average yearly cost for tuition, fees, and living expenses ran around $25,000. Having escaped college with a minimum of student loans, she'd hoped to keep her grad school experience about the same and pay for most of her first year tuition out of pocket. For her second year of school, she planned to use the money she made during a summer job.

One way she opted to save for business school was to live frugally and put away nearly one-third of her take-home pay into a mutual fund. Mutual funds are companies that pool the money of many individuals and invest it into stocks, bonds, and other securities under the guidance of a professional manager. The mutual fund Julie picked billed itself as an "aggressive growth" fund,

which meant that it assumed greater risk to pay out larger returns to its investors. According to the fund literature that Julie read, this particular fund had produced very solid returns over the past 10 years. It had a 17 percent average annual return during the past decade, high by most investing standards (the average stock market return is only around 10 percent annually). Julie figured with this kind of investment growth, her savings earmarked for tuition might nearly double in just over four years, helping offset the need for additional loans.

> **This will not be on the test.** In 1996, the average price for a new car was $18,565, up from $8910 in 1981. The average amount financed for a new car in 1980 was $6322. In 1996, it was $16,988. Along those same lines, the average monthly payment for a new car in 1996 was $404.86, more than double the $183.91 payment 16 years earlier.
> Source: U.S. Department of Commerce, Bureau of Economic Analysis and the American Automobile Manufacturers Association

For three straight years Julie worked at the pharmaceutical firm and dutifully saved her money for grad school. A month before she was set to leave her job and start school, her mutual fund account had grown to $30,000 (the fund had produced an average annual return during those three years of 15 percent). Then it happened.

Four weeks before she started packing for school and fired off a tuition check, the stock market took a nasty fall–a "correction" it was called—dropping nearly 20 percent. Julie's mutual fund reacted even more intensely than the market as a whole, dropping almost 30 percent in value. Overnight, her hard-earned savings had toppled in value from $30,000 to $21,000. That $9000 loss meant that Julie went from being about $5000 ahead of expectations to being about $4000 behind. The result: Julie realized she would probably have to take out a loan to cover her living expenses, something she had hoped to avoid. Unfortunately for Julie, the stock market didn't seem to care much for her graduate school plans.

Saving vs. Investing

What happened to Julie is not meant to frighten would-be investors away from the stock market but rather to make a strong point about the need to understand the important correlation between investments and time and the difference between the need to invest versus the need to save. Investing, by definition, means to make a long-term commitment of putting money away and letting it grow. This involves risk, like downturns in the market, but over the long-term the divots tend to smooth out into a long-term upward growth pattern. Three years is not considered long term, and in the above case, Julie paid the price.

Julie's story illustrates the importance of matching your saving or investing goals with the right tools. As noted before, stocks and stock mutual funds are an excellent long-term investment option. For most of this century, stocks have produced some of the best returns when compared to just about any investment. But in a short time frame, such as under five years, they can burn someone unexpectedly and without remorse. This is akin to people hiking up mountainous terrain. While the elevation may increase along the trail, hikers will probably encounter short drops in elevation, like a ravine or creek, but all the while gain altitude overall. The stock market is no different, except that those financial ravines and creek beds can play havoc on the short-sighted.

So if a long-term commitment to an investment simply isn't possible, as for a person like Julie who's looking to enter graduate school in perhaps three years or someone looking to make a down payment on a new home in two years, there are important financial issues to understand. These issues involve the notion of saving, and preserving, capital.

Whereas investing seeks to make money grow by assuming a certain level of risk and letting it compound, saving seeks to protect the investment capital to make sure that when it's needed, it's both intact and readily accessible.

In Julie's case, her money was accessible in the mutual fund—all she had to do was call the fund and cash out. But while she hit the target on the liquidity issue, she was off-base in the short-term risk category. Her mutual fund was an aggressive growth fund, meaning that while it may have produced high returns historically, it also carried the risk of violently reacting to the market's normal ups and downs. She may have earned a decent return over, say, a ten-year period, but in her three-year period, she was hit by a regular market downturn—an unwelcome but veritable constant.

Julie was correct in recognizing that leaving her money in a non-interest paying checking account was the wrong way to go. It was incorrect however, to assume that much risk with so short an investing horizon.

While she churned in her job, inflation kept eating away the value of her tuition money. Over those two to three years, the savings in a checking account would have eroded, perhaps 6 percent or more based on historical inflation figures. Julie was also aware that she would need her money soon, so she decided not to go with an investment that would have penalized her if she tried to take her money out too early. For example, had she opened a special tax-deferred plan called an Individual Retirement Account for her tuition money, she would have benefited from tax-free growth of her savings, but the day she wanted to pull the money out—if she wasn't age 59 ½ Julie would have been hit by all applicable taxes, as well as a 10 percent early withdrawal penalty. In short, an IRA option would have lost her nearly 40 percent of her savings between the two.

The goal then is to find a way to ensure that money stored for near-term use is safe from risk of loss but also positioned to help offset the insatiable appetite of inflation. To achieve both of these goals, it's important to pick a savings option which does just that, while at the same time is easy to set up, manage, and remove funds from when the time comes. These options, while more complicated than the proverbial cookie jar, will help the investor keep up with inflation at the very least and ensure that when the time comes, the money is there.

Different Savings Options

When deciding where to put money away for a relatively short period of time, you must carefully weigh several factors related to short-term savings. These will dictate which option is best for you, and more important preempt any headaches or cost-intensive mishaps.

The following savings plans can be used individually or in combination—whatever best suits your savings needs. The questions to the left should provide some guidance as to which may best be suited to your particular case.

Short Term Savings Questions

When deciding on short-term savings options, an individual must consider a number of factors including:

- What is the total amount of money that will be placed into this account? *Some savings plans ask for almost nothing to start; others require high minimums to get started or open an account.*

- What's the earliest point at which I will need to access this savings? *While some savings plans allow an individual to yank out his or her money whenever they want, others slap on stiff penalties if the funds are withdrawn before a certain date. Knowing and abiding by these schedules reduces headaches and, more important, the chance of unnecessarily losing money for dumb mistakes.*

- How important is convenience and time in setting up and managing one of these options? *Savings plans run the gamut from ultra-low to somewhat high maintenance, though none require the kind of vigilance that investing does.*

Savings Accounts

Things don't get much simpler than savings accounts. Available at local banks, credit unions, and other financial institutions, these plans allow an individual to open an account with just a basic minimum, often $200 or less. The money earns interest, is readily available to the depositor upon request without penalty, and is usually protected by the Federal Deposit Insurance Corporation (FDIC) up to $100,000.

Of course, the simplicity and protection afforded to savings accounts comes at a cost to the consumer: very low interest payments that barely keep up with inflation. The rates that banks pay on these accounts are dictated by prevailing interest rates and competition and generally do not fluctuate greatly between banks, so shopping around isn't terribly necessary. The factors that decide where to open an account stem more from convenience and cost-saving considerations. For example, a savings account opened where you have a basic checking account may be helpful in providing overdraft protection (a handy little setup that keeps users from bouncing checks and getting penalized by dipping into the savings account funds to cover slight miscalculations). Second, it's smart and easy to have paychecks deposited automatically into these accounts to ensure that a certain amount of money is set aside for savings every month.

CDs

Not to be confused with their musical counterparts, these CDs stand for "certificates of deposit" and can be purchased at banks, credit unions, and brokerage firms. An individual opens a CD with a certain amount of money, often $1000, but sometimes as low as $100, and gets paid a predetermined rate of

CD: Stands for "certificate of deposit." CDs can be purchased at banks, credit unions, and brokerage firms. An individual opens a CD with a certain amount of money, often $1000, but as low as $100, and gets paid a predetermined rate of interest when the CD matures. If the CD is cashed before maturity, the individual is penalized for early withdrawal.

PROFILE

Sally Zink, 27
Tempe, Arizona

In 1996, Sally left her job on the east coast to attend business school at Arizona State University. Realizing years earlier that she was making enough to save a few bucks each month, Sally began planning a way to sock away some cash for her future. After some initial research, Sally opted to park her cash in mutual funds because of their diversification, simplicity, and low costs. She also focused on finding a strong-performing no-load fund to make sure that her investment dollars would not be eaten up by commission costs. Sally looked for funds that would not be a high risk because her tolerance for stomaching the ups and downs of the market was not great. After researching *Morningstar*, a comprehensive mutual fund resource, and a few magazines like *Money* and *Kiplinger's Personal Finance*, Sally contacted a number of mutual fund companies for their prospectuses. Sally eventually chose the no-load Janus Fund (800-525-3713) which she started with just $150. She also chose this company because of its strong reputation and because of the large number of funds within the family of funds (once you are in a mutual fund family, it is easy to switch mutual funds within the family). In addition to the $150 she contributed monthly, Sally occasionally sent in additional bucks, sometimes to the tune of $350 per month. Her mutual fund performed well and by tapping into some of her shares, Sally was able to pay for some of her school expenses during the first year of school without taking a loan. After graduating, Sally hopes to work in the hotel/travel industry and continue pursuing her passion for travelling the globe, of which she is no stranger. Her passport already counts 25 countries on five different continents.

interest when the CD matures. The rate of interest a CD pays is based on a number of factors, including the market rate, competition, and how long until the CD matures. The longer the maturity date, the higher the rate of return.

CDs have a number of advantages and disadvantages for their owners. On the plus side, CDs are federally insured up to $100,000, which means you're guaranteed to get your money back upon maturity. Second, users can determine how much time they have to keep their money, say, one year, and purchase a CD that matches that window.

There are two substantial risks associated with CDs. The first is the rate of return. When money is placed into a CD, it's usually locked in a particular rate of return until maturity. The maturity date may range from 14 days to 10 years, depending on the terms of the CD. The longer it takes the CD to reach maturity, the higher the interest rate paid, because the investor is assuming risk by being locked into a certain rate over a longer time. For example, suppose an investor purchased a three-year CD paying 5 percent interest. If the prevailing interest rate in the market were also 5 percent, that would be a competitive move. But suppose the interest rate crept up to 6 or perhaps 7 percent just after you purchased the CD. Not only is the fund paying less than the newly issued CDs now paying 6 percent, but if you wanted to cash out to buy a new higher-returning CD you'd stumble upon the second risk of CDs—early withdrawal penalties. An investor who attempts to pull her or his money out of a CD before maturity gets slapped with an early withdrawal fee. So attempting to sell the low-interest CD for a higher-interest one may prove unwise and nullify any future gains.

Like shopping around for the best deal on a new stereo, investors can shop around for the highest-paying CDs. Unlike savings accounts, which don't vary widely in the interest rates, CDs may have a larger spread on interest rates. To get the best rates, check the business section of the paper. It generally lists the average CD rates for a region.

Money Market Accounts and Money Market Funds

Think of money market accounts as glorified savings accounts with a cooler name. Money market accounts, like savings accounts, can be opened at most banks and credit unions and may offer an interest rate higher than those of savings accounts. Funds put into these accounts are placed into short-term debt instruments such as CDs and U.S. Treasury bills that mature quickly, often within three months or less. Individuals earn interest on these short-term investments which is paid out weekly or monthly, depending on the institution.

> **Money Market Accounts:** Accounts opened at financial institutions where the money is invested into safe, short-term debt instruments, such as CDs and U.S. Treasury bills. Money market accounts which often allow limited check-writing privledges, often pay a higher return than regular savings accounts.

Money market accounts offer a number of features, such as check-writing privileges, that savings accounts do not. They are also extremely liquid; money can be withdrawn at any time. The downside to money market accounts, however, is that they usually require higher minimum deposits than savings accounts. Most accounts require $1000 to $1500 to get started. Of course, with that higher minimum often come higher returns. Like savings accounts and CDs, the rate of return on a money market account depends upon interest rates. When interest rates go up or down, the return of these accounts follows.

In addition to the money market accounts offered at banks, mutual fund companies offer similar type savings plans called money market funds. Money market funds are invested in the same short-term instruments as money market accounts. They are a smart short-term plan.

By going outside your local branch for a money market fund, you may lose the convenience of one-stop banking. However, most money market funds offer the same services as banks, including check-writing and automatic deposit plans. There is one major benefit of mutual fund-based money accounts over their bank counterparts: total returns. For the most part, mutual funds will offer higher returns on these accounts than banks. The reason has to do with expenses a company incurs known as overhead. Unlike mutual fund companies, banks

Stay Away from that Money

The surest way to squander money is to have it in your hand, and the best way to keep that from happening is to never see it in the first place. To make sure that a short-term savings fund or emergency cash supply remains just that, have the cash from your paycheck deposited directly into your savings, money market account, or money market fund. Most payroll offices allow this to be done for either all or part of your paycheck. Some employees opt to have part of their monthly check sent to their checking accounts to cover bills, whereas a savings-allocated portion goes directly to a money market or savings account. If the payroll system isn't possible, have the funds transferred electronically from your basic checking account or NOW account where your checks are normally deposited. These automatic transfers are free and easy to get started.

often have to maintain large corporate headquarters, numerous regional branches, tellers, and ATM machines. These resources and services aren't free, and the money that keeps them going has to come from some-where—often in the form of lower returns on an account. Since mutual funds don't typically have to pay for such high over-head, the returns on their money market funds tend to be one to several points high-er than their bank competitors.

Like regular mutual funds, money market funds issue shares to the individual. Unlike a regular mutual fund, where the price of a share, its net asset value, fluctu-ates up or down based on the value of the fund's holdings, the value of a money mar-ket fund is maintained at $1 a share. When the fund distributes interest or capital gains on its holdings, the $1 price per share remains stable. Investors either receive a monthly check for these applicable distrib-utions or the money is reinvested to buy more shares at $1 apiece. Money reinvested to purchase more shares generates more income, which in turn can be reinvested to purchase more shares. That's basic compounding.

How to Find a CD or Money Market Fund with the Best Returns: When searching for a certifi-cate of deposit with the highest rate of return, most individuals scan the local newspaper or the neighborhood banks that offer CDs. Trouble is, a newspaper may only keep up with its area's institu-tions, and a bank is only going to have information about its own products. In short, all this searching can become a time-consuming ordeal. Worst of all, the best CDs may not be available at your local bank anyway. That's one reason Roy Henry, cofounder and pres-ident of First Financial Planners in Chesterfield, MO. says to shop via a brokerage firm. Not only do brokers have access to the highest-paying sav-ings instruments nationwide, but if an individual already has an account there, he or she can consolidate all account information—savings and invest-ing—into one statement. Another plus, Henry says, is that CDs purchased through brokers can be sold like any other security, before maturity, without the danger of an early withdrawal fee, while still retaining all the federal insur-ance protections against loss. In addition to brokerage firms, financial journals like *Kiplinger's Personal Finance Magazine* (800-544-0155) list the top-returning CDs and money market funds, along with contact information, every month.

Most major newspapers run daily or weekend updates on the typical rates paid by bank and mutual fund money accounts. You can also call a number of banks or mutual funds directly to get specific information on the accounts. The longer money will be sitting in one of these accounts, the greater impact a higher return may mean.

How Money Market Funds Are Listed

Money market funds are often listed in newspaper and other financial journals in the layout shown below.

1 Name	2 Assets (in billions)	3 Avg. Maturity (in days)	4 7-Day Avg. Yield (%) Current
SchbMM	19.388	61	4.8

1. Fund name, in this case the abbreviated name for Schwab Money Market.

2. Assets denote the total amount of money held in this fund ($19.39 billion).

3. The average maturity indicates how long, on average, investments in the money market fund have until they mature. Longer maturities are favorable when interest rates are dropping because they allow the fund to hold onto higher paying instruments longer. However, longer maturity rates are a disadvantage when interest rates are climbing because the fund is stuck with lower interest paying holdings. For this fund, it's 61 days.

4. The yield is the interest earned on the fund (either listed as a 7-day or monthly rate) and given at an annual rate (APR). For the Schwab Money Market fund, the current yield is 4.8 percent.

Mutual Funds

Mutual funds, by their very design, are a safer investment than buying individual stocks and bonds (For more information on mutual funds, check out Chapter 3, which is completely devoted to them.) Since an individual's money is first pooled with that of thousands of others, then invested into several, even hundreds of different securi-

---

Different Categories of Mutual Funds

Higher returns are married to higher risk when it comes to investing. So when considering whether to park some cash for short-term savings into mutual funds, understanding this concept is key. Put your money into the wrong type of fund, such as aggressive growth or international stock funds, and you could be saying good-bye to some or all of that soon-to-be-needed cash if the market goes south. That's one reason financial experts say, for short-term savings, bond funds make sense. While bond funds may never achieve the kind of returns desirable for a long-term investment plan, they do the trick when it comes to the here and now. That's because bonds, known as fixed-income securities, virtually guarantee a certain return over a given period a time. That's something that stocks cannot do.

Categories of mutual funds range from the safe and low returns to riskier but higher returns. A breakdown of those groups is as follows:

Aggressive Growth: Combines several investing strategies to capture greater returns.
Small Company Funds: Often invests in stock of small companies that could take off.
International Stock Funds: Puts money into the stock of foreign corporations.
Sector Funds: Money is invested into one industry of stocks, such as technology.

Growth Funds: Invests into stocks with a long history of growth and stock price increases.
Growth and Income Funds: Invests in both dividend stocks and bonds.

Bond Funds: Money is invested into corporate, government, or municipal bonds.

High short-term risk
Medium short-term risk
Low short-term risk

---

ties, the chance of losing money is greatly diminished. That protection comes from the investing principle known as diversification, or spreading the money among many different investments to protect against loss in any one.

Some kinds of mutual funds are an attractive savings option for the short-term investor as well. With easy setup procedures and automatic monthly deposits taken directly from a checking account, mutual funds are a low-maintenance way to put money for savings directly into an account without having to cut a check or dig up a stamp. Furthermore, simple monthly statements and high liquidity are ideal for someone to track and take their savings as needed.

Like any investment, however, mutual funds always carry an element of risk—and obviously, some funds are riskier than others. The level of risk that a fund will subject its investors to is directly tied to the objectives, or goals, of the fund. A fund that seeks aggressive growth for its investors might place its money into the stocks of smaller, younger companies that may flourish or may crash and burn. Other funds aim simply to protect the capital of the investor while securing a small bit of income to offset the impact of inflation. These are the funds an individual who has a short-term savings window needs to understand and seek out.

Financial planners recommend a different category of mutual funds for people looking to save for three years or less. Funds falling into this category offer a high level of protection against loss of principal and also provide some income to offset the erosion factors of inflation.

Corporate Bond Funds

These funds invest money into corporate bonds that seek a high-level of income. The bonds the fund chooses are generally safe picks, and the company that issues them will most likely be able to pay up come maturity time. Investors in bond funds do, however, deal with another kind of risk, interest rate risk.

Government Bond Funds

Government bond funds are invested in the debts of local, municipal, and federal government. These bonds, which are backed by either the taxing power of the state or some other revenue source, are generally safe and provide stable returns. One additional benefit is that some investments into municipal bonds enable the investor to receive income that is exempt from federal, and sometimes state taxes.

Global Bond Funds

In addition to the bonds issued by the government of the United States, there are also bonds issued by companies and governments worldwide. After all, all governments need revenue. Global bond funds invest in the bonds of companies that are located overseas as well as in the United States.

BOY, I COULD USE PROFESSIONAL HELP WITH MY FINANCES

Make no mistake, monetary decisions are never easy, and the choices between where, how, and when to save just seem to get more complicated over time. New products are constantly hitting the market that offer better returns and fewer hassles. Keeping up with this armada of offerings can be a drag. Staying informed of all the available savings options is a great first step, but if you still think you need more help–or feel overwhelmed by the process–you can always turn to the experts and have them manage your money. These financial professionals can help you create money management plans for a short-term crunch, such as paying off loans or other debts, or long-term goals like saving for retirement. Their fee schedules may range from a flat sum for services to a percentage of the assets they manage.

Financial Professionals:
The National Association of Personal Financial Advisors
http://www.napfa.org
(888) 333-6659

International Association of Registered Financial Consultants
(800) 532-9060

International Association for Financial Planning
(800) 945-4237

American Association of Individual Investors
http://www.aaii.org
(312) 280-0170
This Chicago-based nonprofit group helps people get started in investing, and has available a hefty book on no-load mutual funds. Their site offers lots of free information and advice on getting started.

National Association of Investors Corporation (NAIC)
http://www.better-investing.org/
(810) 583-6242
Get the details on how to start your own investment club–a group of individuals that meets regularly to collectively pool their money and pick securities in which to invest. Ever hear of the Beardstown Ladies?

Q.u.i.c.k. D.o.w.n.l.o.a.d.

- Saving is the protection and preservation of money, or capital, from loss.

- Savings is a strategy to use when your money will be needed within a fairly short time frame, perhaps three years or less. Investing is not a wise money management option when the time horizon is this short. In these cases there is a strong chance for loss of the investment, particularly in the stock market, which historically has experienced short-term drops in value.

- There are a number of factors to consider when selecting a savings plan. Some of these include (1) how much money you will put into this account, (2) how much time before these funds are needed, and (3) how much convenience is a factor.

- There are a number of different savings options to explore, each with its own benefits and drawbacks. Four major types include savings accounts, certificates of deposit (CDs), money market accounts, and certain bond mutual funds.

- One way to get the best rates of return on saving instruments like CDs and money market funds is through stockbrokers, who have access to information on these instruments nationwide.

 # Plaid Trousers in the Sun: Investing for Retirement

The future's so bright I gotta wear shades.—Timbuk3

Future Shock

Imagine needing to come up with a cool $2 million overnight. Not likely, right? But if you expect to retire at age 65 and live comfortably through your retirement years, you will need that much or more on the day you join the ranks of the Florida-bound. True, you might be able to expect a little help from the government through a federal entitlement program like Social Security, but face it, the real burden of saving falls on the individual. So while that seven-figure nestegg seems daunting, remember this: You can have your $2 million retirement nestegg by starting to save now with a whopping $25 a week. Read on and we'll explain some practical—and painless—ways how.

"The future's So Bright I Gotta Wear Shades," IRS Music. Used by permission.

Don't Blow It Off

Since previous generations could count on collecting fairly generous Social Security and Medicare benefits during their retirement years, the incentive to invest and save for retirement was not as compelling as it is today. It's no secret that the United States is aging and doing it rather quickly. In 1900, one in 25 Americans was over 65. In 2040, one in 4 Americans will be over 65. The 85-plus generation will triple in the next 50 years. This demographic time bomb means additional strains on the social programs designed to help the elderly and less of a chance that younger generations will benefit from these programs. This means that our generation must assume the responsibility of being able to support ourselves in retirement, with little or no help from the government.

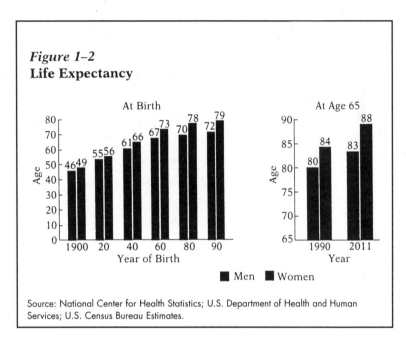

Figure 1–2
Life Expectancy

At Birth

At Age 65

Source: National Center for Health Statistics; U.S. Department of Health and Human Services; U.S. Census Bureau Estimates.

Financial experts differ on what percentage of preretirement income you will need during retirement to maintain a standard of living comparable to that of your working years, but most agree that the percentage is somewhere between 70 and 90 percent. And that money will have to last for a significant amount of time. Americans are living much longer than they used to, sometimes planning on spending 20 years or more in retirement. That means you'll need to

THE YOUNG AND THE WISE

Polls taken by *USA Today* and the Roper Organization show that eight out of ten 19- to 30-year-olds are counting on personal savings to bankroll their retirement. Only about half of baby boomers expressed that expectation when they were in their twenties.

accumulate that much more in savings between now and the day you retire to support yourself during those years.

Under current conditions, Social Security, the federal program that provides benefits to workers through their retirement, will reach bankruptcy by approximately 2029. The federal Medicare program, which provides health care for America's senior citizens, is projected to go bankrupt much sooner; current estimates indicate it will go belly up soon after the turn of the century. Although politicians will not let these programs disappear, benefits in the future will certainly be scaled back from their current level. And even if you are banking on Social Security to be around, it currently pays the average retirees only about 40 percent of their pre-retirement salaries.

If you are interested in calculating what your Social Security benefits will be under current law, the Social Security Administration has a worksheet they will send you by calling (800) 772-1213, or you can order it through their web site at *http://www.ssa.gov*.

POP GOES THE CULTURE

The twentysomething advocacy group Third Millennium found that those between the ages of 18 and 34, by a majority of 53 percent to 34 percent, expect the soap opera *General Hospital* to outlast the Medicare program. An earlier survey by the same group found that just over one-fourth of people between similar ages believed Social Security will still exist when they retire, compared with 46 percent who believe in UFOs.

What It All Means

Preaching and soothsaying aside, all these factors point to an urgent need for current and successive generations to take charge of their financial future and carry the burden of personal savings. Washington has noticed too. Beginning in the late 1970s, Congress recognized the need for increasing personal retirement savings, and legislation was passed making it easier for individuals to save for retirement. Two of the ways in which the government has provided incentives to save money for the longterm are through employer-sponsored retirement plans, commonly referred to as 401(k) plans, and through Individual Retirement Accounts (IRAs). Both of these investment vehicles are great deals and are worth learning about.

Demographic Meltdown

In 1945 there were about 42 workers for each Social Security beneficiary. By 1990 that ratio has fallen to about 3.4:1 today, and by 2020 there will only be 2.4 workers for every beneficiary.

Source: OASDI Board of Trustees, 1996.

401(K) PLANS
Some Quick Background

One of the best and most popular ways to save for retirement is through what's called an "employer-sponsored retirement plan." These plans often have technical sounding names like 401(k) and 403(b). For lack of a better title, they were simply labeled after the section of the federal tax code that allows them to exist. The best known and most prevalent of these plans is the 401(k) plan. These plans were created by Congress in 1978 to encourage employees and employers to jointly share the responsibility of saving for retirement.

More retirement plans. Depending on what type of organization you work for, you may come across a number of 401(k)-style plans that were also established in the behemoth U.S. tax code. The 403(b) was established for employees of religious, charitable, educational, research organizations, and cultural agencies. The largest of these 403(b) plans is known as the Teachers Insurance Annuity Association/College Retirement Equity Fund, TIAA-CREF (http://www.tiaa-cref.org/). Other plans include Section 457 plans, which apply to state and local governments; SEP's, Keogh's, and SIMPLE plans were designed for small businesses and the self-employed. Although there are several different plans, we will refer to them generically for the rest of the chapter as 401(K) plans. However, in certain circumstances, there may be differences. Therefore, you should always check the specifics of your plan as well as consult with someone in the human resources and/or benefits department with any questions.

What Exactly Is This 401(k) Thing Anyway?

A *401(k) plan* is a retirement plan that allows employees to contribute a portion of their paychecks to a company investment plan until retirement or termination of service from the company. A worker can save money through his or her company for retirement by diverting a certain amount of compensation from their paycheck *tax-deferred*, a beneficial setup in which taxes are not paid on this savings until much later down the road.

The 401(k) plan, also known in broader terms as a "defined-contribution plan," varies from more traditional pension plans, which are known as "defined-benefit plans." A defined-benefit plan pays workers at a fixed rate after retirement, normally based on a percentage of salary and number of years of service. Under defined-benefit plans, the employer chooses how to invest the money and therefore bears the investment risk. (As will be explained shortly, this differs from a 401(k)-type plan where the *employee* selects how the money is to be invested). Defined-benefit plans turn out to be pretty useless for someone who changes jobs frequently (it is hard to build up any substantial savings with any one employer), and over the past 20 years, the trend has shifted heavily from defined benefit to 401(k)-style defined-contribution plans.

Although 401(k) plans were created through federal legislation, decisions about establishment as well as administration are made by the individual, and in fact, employers are not required to offer such plans at all. The government has simply set the outline and broad rules about tax status, etc., for companies to go ahead and set them up. One thing is for sure, the earlier you start, the easier it will be to accumulate a significant stash for retirement.

401(k) plan: An employer sponsored retirement plan that allows employees to contribute to a company investment plan, before taxes are taken out, until retirement or termination of service from the company.

Tax-deferred: The ability to put off paying taxes on your investment until some time in the future.

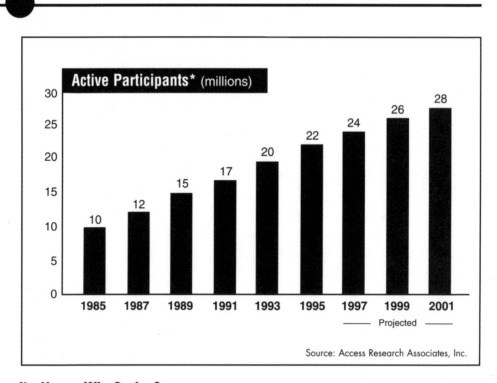

Active Participants* (millions)

Source: Access Research Associates, Inc.

I'm Young. Why Bother?

If you work for a company that offers a 401(k) plan, the arguments for participating are simply overwhelming. But for those needing additional convincing, a few of the major considerations are:

Escaping the Tax Man

The first big advantage lies in the concept of tax-deferral. The money that goes into a 401(k) plan is taken from your paycheck *before* taxes are deducted. By not taxing the money contributed into your plan, the government provides you with a tremendous compounding advantage to let that money grow throughout your working years. Of course, Uncle Sam will eventually take his part, but it won't be until later, and by this time you will have recognized a huge advantage from having this money invested and grow. There are a few immediate advantages of tax deferral which at first may not be obvious.

1. The first advantage is that your taxable income can be greatly reduced by contributing to a tax-deferred plan. Consider the following: If you have a $30,000 annual salary and contribute $2000 of your income to your retirement plan, your federal taxable income drops to $28,000 before factoring other deductions and exemptions. Therefore, the more you contribute to a tax-deferred account, as opposed to, let's say, a regular savings account, which would be post-taxed dollars, the more

> **Are you eligible?** If you are 21 years old, and have been with an employer for a year, you are generally eligible to enroll in their 401(k) plan. Employers can't make the waiting period more than this, and it may even be less. All information about specifics should be readily available from someone in your human resources and/or benefits department.

your tax burden is reduced. If you contribute generously, this could provide a significant reduction in your tax bill compared to someone making a comparable salary and contributing to a non-tax-deferred plan such as a savings account (see worksheet on following page). Furthermore, the money inside a tax-deferred account is allowed to grow tax-free. This differs from ordinary savings accounts or investments, which require that taxes be paid on interest or dividend income as it is accrued. By not taxing this growth, a 401(k)-style plan is allowed to grow and compound faster than a retirement account that is taxable.

2. Because 401(k) contributions are taken from paychecks before they are taxed, the real reduction on take-home pay might not be as much as you think. Consider someone with a $30,000 salary who would be paid $2500 monthly. That income is going to be reduced by federal, state, local and other applicable taxes to the tune of maybe $750 (about 30 percent) per month. That means the take-home would be only $1750 in this case. If that person were to contribute 5 percent of her salary to a 401(k), $125 would be taken off the initial $2500 before any federal taxes were taken out. Therefore, only $2375 would be subject to federal taxes, reducing the overall tax. So after all is said and done, the total take-home might drop by about $90, less than the actual $125 that went to the retirement account.

<table>
<tr><td>

This will not be on the test. In 1997 the average American worked 128 days — from January 1 to May 8 — satisfy all federal, state, and local tax obligations for the year. On average, Americans spend 2 hours and 49 minutes of each working day laboring to pay taxes.

Source: The Tax Foundation

</td></tr>
</table>

Free Money–Employer Match

Many employers will agree to kick some money into your retirement plan. This is known as a "matching contribution." For the record, these matching contributions aren't just some kind of altruistic corporate freebie: They are tax-deductible business expenses for the company's bottom line as well.

Employers vary on if and how much they are willing to contribute. This amount can range from partial to full matching to even over-matching of the employee contribution. An employer may choose to match 100 percent for every dollar an employee contributes up to maybe 6 percent of the employee's salary. This would mean that for every dollar you contribute to your account, your employer would also kick in a dollar up to 6 percent of your salary. If your salary was $30,000 and you contributed 6 percent, or $150 a month, the company would match that $150 making your total monthly contribution $300. Again, the specifics of your company's plan will be available from someone in your human resources and/or benefits department.

	RETIREMENT PLAN	EXAMPLE	SAVINGS ACCOUNT	EXAMPLE
your base salary	$_____	$ 30,000	$_____	$ 30,000
your pretax contribution	-$_____	-$ 2,000	-$_____0_____	-$ 0
your taxable income	=$_____	=$ 28,000	=$_____	=$ 30,000
30% tax rate (assumed for all federal and state taxes)	x_____	x .30	x_____	x .30
your total taxes	=$_____	=$ 8,400	=$_____	=$ 9,000
your take-home pay (income - taxes)	=$_____	$ 19,600	=$_____	$ 21,000
your "savings account" contribution	-$_____0_____	-$ 0	-$_____	-$ 2,000
your spendable income	=$_____	=$ 19,600	=$_____	=$ 19,000

In the example, the person saving in a retirement plan takes home **$600 more** than the person saving outside plan.

Source: T. Rowe Price Associates, Inc. Reprinted by permission.

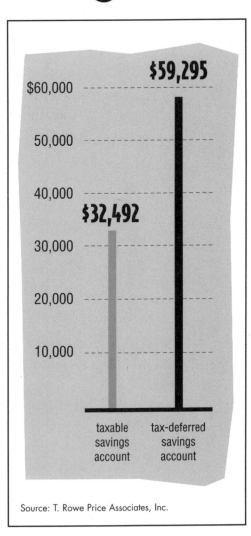

$59,295

$60,000

50,000

40,000

$32,492

30,000

20,000

10,000

taxable savings account | tax-deferred savings account

Source: T. Rowe Price Associates, Inc.

It's not often in the investing world that someone gives you free money—risk free. That's why an employer's matching contribution represents the single best investment return available anywhere. There simply is nothing that allows investors to instantly receive a 50, 75, or even 100 percent return on their money instantly, like there is with a 401(k) plan.

But there is a catch. In order to keep the money your employer has contributed, you are re-quired to work at that company for a specific period of time. This time commitment is determined by the employer and is usually between one and seven years. The right of the employee to keep the money the company has contributed is called vesting. An employer will generally use one of two types of vesting schedules.

Cliff vesting is when you can keep 100 percent of the employer-contributed money at the end of a predetermined length of service, say five years. Graded vesting is when you gradually become vested between a certain number of years. In some cases you may become vested 20 percent each year until you

> **Vesting:** The right, which an employee gradually acquires through length of service, to receive employer-contributed benefits to a retirement plan. Vesting can happen one of two ways: **Cliff vesting** occurs when you can keep 100 percent of employer contributions at the end of a predetermined length of service. **Graded vesting** is when one you become vested between a certain number of years. You may become vested 20 percent each year until you eventually reach 100 percent.

PROFILE

Beth Darcy, 27
Vass, North Carolina

What should you do with your 401(k) money when you change jobs? Beth Darcy confronted that question when she left her job in 1995. For three and a half years, Beth socked away a portion of her salary into the plan and was well on her way toward a sizable retirement nest egg. When she left her job, Beth had accumulated almost $10,000 and had to decide between leaving the money in the present account or transferring the funds into a special roll-over Individual Retirement Account (IRA). She opted against cashing out of her plan because that would have subjected her to heavy taxation and an early withdrawal penalty. Unsatisfied with her existing 401(k) investment options, Beth decided to move those funds into an IRA mutual fund with better returns. Using sources such as *Morningstar* and *The Wall Street Journal*, Beth narrowed her choices from the thousands of funds on the market and finally decided on the Harbor Capital Appreciation Fund (800-422-1050). "This fund gave me the opportunity to beat the market, rather than just keep pace," she says. Beth plans on using this money for retirement savings. Beth and her husband Chris—who enjoy golf, mountain biking, and fly-fishing—have also invested some money into international and small-cap mutual funds on the side. They've also opened an on-line trading account to purchase some blue chip stocks and enroll in their Dividend Reinvestment Plans (DRIPs). This variety of investments allows them to allocate their assets across different risk and return categories and helps them remain diversified. "We invest to cover our retirement needs, as well as shorter-term investments which we plan to use to buy furniture and other necessities when we purchase a house." One of the best parts: They like investing: "We have developed a great interest that we probably spend more time on than any of the other hobbies we share," they say.

eventually reach 100 percent, meaning you keep all of the employer's contributions. Suppose this was the arrangement with your employer. If you left the job after, say, two years and were 40 percent vested, that means you would own all of your contributions, plus 40 percent of what the company had matched. This is a very important point to understand about vesting: No matter what happens with the employer's contributions, your own contributions are *always* 100 percent fully vested from the time you start a 401(k) plan.

Young blood. Of the 5 million people who started businesses in 1995, nearly 800,000 were under the age of 25. More than 1.5 million had not yet reached their 30th birthday. Another half million in their twenties—or even younger—bought existing businesses.

Source: National Federation of Independent Business

Hassle-Free Automatic Deductions/Contributions

Another feature of employer-sponsored retirement plans is that contributions can come directly out of your paycheck and are deposited into your 401(k) account. It takes discipline and determination to be a successful long-term investor, and with a 401(k) plan that process is made much easier through automatic deductions. There's no need to send a check at the beginning of each month. That's a good thing, too, because the temptation may be too great to simply put it off a given month because of any one of a thousand excuses (i.e., "I'm expecting a lot of expenses this month." "I'll just wait until next month." "My cat ate the checkbook, again."). So, conveniently, money can be taken directly from your paycheck and placed into your 401(k) plan without any real effort.

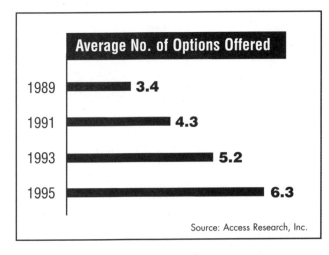

Average No. of Options Offered

1989	3.4
1991	4.3
1993	5.2
1995	6.3

Source: Access Research, Inc.

Where Does My Money Go?

Each month, when contributions are made to your retirement plan, your employer deposits them into your individual account. The money is then invested in any number of options—mutual funds, money markets, or company stock to name a few. This choice will be offered to you when you enroll in the plan. When filling out the original paperwork, chances are you will

have more than one investment option. If more than one option is offered, it's up to you to determine how to invest it in your account. In 1995 the average number of investment choices offered by a company was 6.3 and that number is nearly double the number in 1989. Keep in mind that along with the responsibility of choosing where to invest your money, you will also shoulder the risks of these investments.

In order to make an informed decision about investment choices, you should be aware of the implications of these different choices.

Reviewing this type of information is key because funds can vary greatly. Aggressive growth mutual funds, for example, seek to maximize capital gains (an increase in the value of an asset) with little interest or dividends (income). They often invest in young companies which have the potential for huge growth. Growth mutual funds invest in the common stock of well-established companies. They seek capital gain with just a small emphasis on current income. Growth & Income funds invest in companies that can increase in value but also have an established record of paying dividends. International mutual funds invest in securities that are traded overseas. Investment value fluctuates in international funds not only because of investment worth but also because of foreign currency exchange rates. Bond funds invest in corporate and government bonds. Sector/Specialty funds invest in particular sectors like energy or technology. (For more information on mutual funds, refer back to Chapter 3.)

> One of the likely investment choices you'll have in a 401(k) plan is mutual funds. If faced with the decision of what type of mutual fund to choose, you should know the different types of funds and their objectives. Literature and information that comes with the 401(k) application should describe each of the funds, including its objectives, risks, and past performance. Also, see Chapter 3 for a full discussion of mutual funds.

Expert Corner

Advice on your 401(k). Two important questions that arise when a new employee starts a 401(k) plan are (1) How much should I contribute? and (2) Into which mutual funds, if given a choice, should those dollars go? Put in as much as money the company will match, says Steve Bailey, a Charlotte, North Carolina-based registered financial consultant with over 20 years in the business. Check with your company, but most employers will match 25 cents to one dollar on the dollar up to around 6 percent of your salary. If a company matches dollar for dollar, you're automatically getting 100 percent on your investment with no risk. "It's hard to match that kind of guaranteed return on your money anywhere," Bailey says. As to which funds to pick if given a choice, Bailey encourages creating a mixed bag of higher-and lower-risk funds, based on your age. To calculate your mix, he suggests subtracting your age, say 25, from 100. That number, 75 in this case, would be the percentage of your money that should go into higher-risk investments, such as growth mutual funds. The remaining amount — 25 percent in this case could be placed into a more conservative investment, like a bond mutual fund. As a rule, Bailey says an individual should not invest money into more than four funds. More than four means the individual may lose some of the power of compounding.

You may also have the option of investing in the stock of the company you work for. Most financial advisors agree that investing in the stock of the company you work for is risky because of a lack of diversification. It places your retirement planning in the hands of one company. And if the stock of that company should drop or falter for any reason, say good-bye to sunny Florida and those baggy plaid trousers. Moreover, you could lose your job in the same downturn.

Starting a Plan

You won't get any perks like a clock radio or free steak knives just for signing up (except maybe a chance at joining the millionaire's club), but at least the forms are no more complicated than filling out an application for a credit card. On the following page is a sample application from *U.S. News & World Report*, where the employee has the option of choosing between 13 different mutual funds from Fidelity Investments.

Among the most important decisions when starting a 401(k) plan is determining how much of your salary to contribute to the plan. In 1997 the dollar limit for an individual to contribute is $9500 a year of pretax dollars, which is raised in $500 increments every so often to reflect inflation. Some employers allow you to make additional

**U.S. News & World Report/The Atlantic Monthly
401(k) PLAN INITIAL CONTRIBUTION AGREEMENT**

The Atlantic

The 401(k) Plan is designed to give employees a means to save for their future financial needs. You may elect to contribute from 1% to 10% (in whole percentages), or the maximum annual deferral set by the IRS, whichever is less, in both pre-tax and after-tax dollars. Your company will make a matching contribution of 75 cents for each dollar of the first 6% of your salary you elect to defer.

The Provisions of the 401(k) Plan are explained in the Summary Plan Description.

You may change the percentage of salary you elect to defer at any time by submitting a Contribution Change Form at least 2 weeks prior to the effective date of the change.

Last Name (Please print)   First Name   Middle Initial

Home Address   City   State   Zip Code

Soc. Sec. No.   Date of Birth mo/day yr   Effective date mo/day/yr

Send statements _____ Office _____ Home _____

Date of Employment   Vesting Date

❑ I wish to join the Plan. I have indicated below the percentage of my salary I would like the company to deduct from my paycheck, and authorize the company to contribute these amounts to the Plan on my behalf.

_____ % in Pre-tax Dollars   _____ % in After-tax Dollars

Contributions to be invested in the funds checked in the amount (as a percentage) as indicated. (Increments of 10%)

❑ Retirement Government Money Market Portfolio _____ %
❑ Retirement Money Market Portfolio _____ %
❑ Fidelity Growth & Income Portfolio _____ %
❑ Fidelity Capital Appreciation Fund _____ %
❑ Fidelity Overseas Fund _____ %

❑ Fidelity Intermediate Bond Fund _____ %
❑ Fidelity Real Estate Investment Portfolio _____ %
❑ Fidelity Magellan Fund _____ %
❑ Fidelity Growth Company Fund _____ %

❑ Fidelity Puritan Fund _____ %
❑ Fidelity U.S. Equity Index Portfolio _____ %
❑ Fidelity Europe Fund _____ %
❑ Fidelity Asset Manager _____ %

The Employer's match portion of your account will be invested in the Retirement Money Market Portfolio until you become 100% vested. After you are 100% vested, the Employer's match will remain in the Retirement Money Market Portfolio unless you call Fidelity directly to instruct them to move the Employer's match into other funds.

I understand that as my salary increases, the amount contributed will also increase. The percentage contributed will remain the same.

Employee's Signature   Date

401(k) Plan Administrator   Date

Note: This designation is to be made in duplicate; one copy to be filed with Personnel, D.C., Rm. 100, and the other copy to be returned to the individual.

Source: U.S. News & World Report. Reprinted by permission.

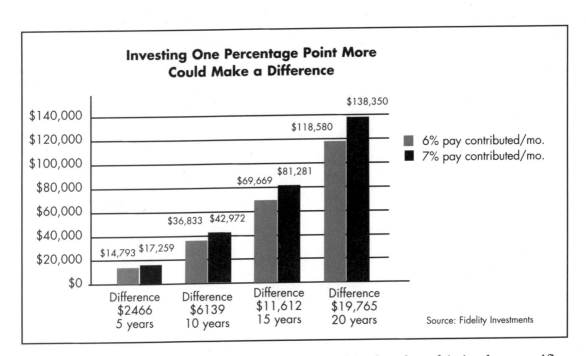

Investing One Percentage Point More Could Make a Difference

6% pay contributed/mo.
7% pay contributed/mo.

$138,350
$118,580
$81,281
$69,669
$42,972
$36,833
$17,259
$14,793

$140,000
$120,000
$100,000
$80,000
$60,000
$40,000
$20,000
$0

Difference $2466 5 years
Difference $6139 10 years
Difference $11,612 15 years
Difference $19,765 20 years

Source: Fidelity Investments

after-tax contributions to your 401(k) plan, but this is plan specific. These after-tax contributions are more accessible down the road for early withdrawals but miss some of the advantages of tax-deferred contributions. Total contributions, including employer and employee, pretax and after-tax, cannot exceed 25 percent of pay or $30,000, whichever is lower. The amount you decide to contribute is your call, but keep in mind that over time even one percentage point can make a big difference. For instance, over the long run the difference between a 6 percent and 7 percent contribution of a $40,000 average salary over 20 years can amount to almost $20,000. This becomes even more if you add in for employer contributions. (See chart.)

Another major decision you may have to make when enrolling is where you want your money to be invested during your working years. The whole point of enrolling in a retirement plan is that your money grows during your working years by being invested for you by your employer. So while you slave away and diligently contribute to the plan, your company does the best it can to make sound investment decisions. Most likely, you will have a say in where your money goes.

Your choice of which type of mutual fund or other investment option to invest in comes down to a balance of risk versus reward. An aggressive growth mutual fund has a much higher risk factor but also has the potential to produce handsome results. According to Ibbotson Associates, a Chicago-based investment research firm, stocks have, over time, provided investors with the best returns. In fact, since 1926, small company stocks, the ones you might find in aggressive growth funds, have posted an average annual return of 12.6 percent, over seven points higher than long-term government bonds. If you are interested in testing your stomach for risk and have not already done so, turn back to Chapter 1 and complete the Investor Risk Quiz on page 12. Also, refer

LESS RISK
Money market funds
Bond funds
Income or balanced funds
Growth and income funds
Growth funds
Aggressive growth funds
Company stock
MORE RISK

Impact of 2% Increase in Return

While Working: 43% Increase in Accumulation (After 30 Years)

Investment Vehicle	Annual Contribution	Assumed Rate of Return	Value After 30 Years
Balanced* Portfolio	$2,000	%8	$226,566
Fixed-Income Portfolio	$2,000	%6	$158,116

Source: Fidelity Investments

to the side chart to see a ranking of volatility based on investment objective, from least volatile to most.

Keep in mind that long-term investments have more time to weather any stock market fluctuations, and the extra percentage you could get from an aggressive growth fund as opposed to a bond mutual fund can make a real difference when talking about a 20- or 30-year investment window. Consider the preceeding chart which shows the difference between an 6 percent and a 7 percent return on the same investment over a period of 20 years.

Accessing Your Money

Retirement plans were created as an incentive to save for the long term, and therefore, they make it difficult for you to cash out your 401(k) plan. At 59½ you are allowed to start making withdrawals without paying any early withdrawal penalties. The law requires you to begin withdrawals at age 70½, regardless of circumstances. When this time comes, you will have to make important decisions about your cashing out strategy, but in general, you will be able to receive a lump-sum distribution or a lifetime annuity—a series of monthly checks, or several withdrawals over a period of time.

Hardship Withdrawals

One of the obvious concerns about starting a 401(k) plan is the question of accessing that money in the case of dire need, such as a medical emergency. Should you find yourself in a financial pinch, many plans allow for what is known as a "hardship withdrawal." These apply only in extreme circumstances (the IRS does not count the need for a new Jeep Wrangler as an extreme circumstance). Most companies allow for hardship withdrawals. According to the most recent survey from the Profit Sharing/401(k) Council of America about 84 percent of plans allow for hardship withdrawals. In order to qualify for these withdrawals you must be able to prove that a financial hardship exists and that there are not any other resources available to you to handle that financial need. Although your company may have its own guidelines on hardship withdrawals, the tax code specifically recognizes four hardships. They are:

- Unreimbursable medical expenses
- Purchase of a primary residence
- Payment of post-secondary tuition for you or a dependent for the next year
- To prevent eviction from or foreclosure on your home

\<Online Info\>

Retirement sites on the web:

Fidelity Investments
http://www.fidelityatwork.com
Focuses specifically on retirement issues. Includes many frequently asked questions as well as a retirement planning calculator. Also includes recent market overviews.

American Savings Education Council
http://www.asec.org
A coalition of public and private groups that seek to raise awareness about retirement. One site highlight: Top 10 ways to beat the clock and prepare for retirement.

Retirement & Savings Directory
http://www.savingsnet.com/
Links and information on everything from insurance and investment basics to Social Security and estate planning.

Employee Benefit Research Institute
http://www.ebri.org
A nonprofit group that provides original and nonpartisan research on a variety of issues affecting retirement and benefit programs.

Self-Employed? Here's What You Should Know

With many young people starting their own businesses, the question of how to save for retirement presents an interesting dilemma. While Individual Retirement Accounts are designed to help people store away that long-term nest egg, they have an annual contribution limit of just $2000 per year. That's much smaller than the current limits of $9500 for 401(k) plans at larger firms. The issue then becomes how to begin saving a sufficient amount for your retirement for yourself as well as provide a savings plan for your employees. There are some options which the government has created for those who don't work for the IBMs and P&Gs of the world. The first of these options is the Simplified Employee Pension, or SEP. If you are self-employed, a SEP plan allows you and those who work for you to set up an individual retirement account with a maximum yearly contribution of 15 percent of pay or $30,000, whichever is less. Employees must be included if they are 21, have worked for you in at least three of the immediately preceding five years, and receive at least $400 in compensation. All funds are immediately vested as well as subject to the same penalties for early distributions as IRAs. On January 1, 1997, a new type of plan came into existence known as Savings Incentive Match Plans for Employees (SIMPLE) for employers with 100 or fewer employees. There are actually two types of SIMPLE plans, (1) SIMPLE retirement accounts, and (2) SIMPLE 401(k) plans, which operate under special rules designed to help small businesses. Under the retirement account version an employee may contribute a percentage of salary on a tax-deferred basis up to $6000 a year. Employers are required to contribute at either 2 percent of pay or a match of the employees contributions up to 3 percent. SIMPLE 401(k) plans require the employer to meet similar contribution requirements as the SIMPLE retirement account. These plans also cap employee contributions at $6000 per year. If you are a small-business owner, most financial institutions should be able to help you set up these plans. Also, for the self-employed, more complicated Keogh plans are also available. These can be set up only by a sole proprietor or a partnership. For more information on these plans, check out the Internal Revenue Service's Publication 560, call (800) 829-3676, or check out their website at http://www.irs.gov.

Hardship withdrawals are subject to both a 10 percent early withdrawal penalty as well as all applicable taxes, which can take a huge cut out of the savings pot. For example, to walk away with $35,000, assuming a 25 percent tax rate and a 10 percent withdrawal penalty, you would have to withdrawal $54,000 from your plan.

There are certain circumstances in which you would be exempt from the 10 percent penalty and only owe taxes. These are:

• You have reached 59½
• Severance of service from company if over the age of 55
• Disability
• Death

Home a Loan

According to the Profit Sharing/401(k) Council of America, about 84 percent of 401(k) plans allow employees to take loans from their plans. This allows borrowing from your 401(k) account and paying the money back into your account—with interest. The money you borrow is not subject to any early withdrawal penalties as long the loan is paid back within the guidelines established with your employer. Normally, employers allow employees to borrow at a fairly low rate of interest. If you have to take a loan from your account, the amount is normally capped at either 50 percent of your vested balance or $50,000, minus any loans you already have outstanding, whichever is less.

Before taking a loan from your plan keep in mind that there are consequences if you do not fulfill your end of the bargain. Specifics of taking a loan will be set by your company, and you should be well aware of the rules as well as the consequences of

Temp Nation

Between an individual's 18th and 30th birthdays, he or she will hold an average of 7.5 jobs. Over a quarter have held 10 or more jobs, while fewer than 1 in 5 have held 3 or fewer jobs.

Source: U.S. Department of Labor, Bureau of Labor Statistics, National Longitudinal Surveys.

default. But if you follow the rules in doing so, you can enjoy a couple of solid benefits by borrowing from yourself rather than a bank. First, the interest rate applied to your own payback is generally lower than that of banks. And for larger loans, that can make a huge difference over time. Second, when paying interest to a bank, that's simply lost money, a cost of borrowing. When paying back a 401(k) loan, all interest, as well as the principal, goes back to you. So even though you technically pay interest on the loan, it's all going back to the same pot, yours.

Bye Bye Job

The days of working for a single company for 30 years seem to be over. There are several options available regarding 401(k) plans and changing employers.

Option 1: Leave your money where it is. Most plans should allow this option. However, they will probably not allow you to add additional money to your stash, and this should be reason enough to steer away from this option.

Option 2: Roll the money over into another retirement plan. If you are going to a new employer immediately, you can arrange for a rollover that will transfer your 401(k) plan from one employer to another without being subject to any type of penalty or tax.

Option 3: Roll your money into an Individual Retirement Account, or IRA (explained later in this chapter). If you choose to do this, you should arrange for a direct roll over between your old employer and the IRA trustee. This keeps it safe from any tax burdens. You can then keep this money in an IRA until you want to move into a new employer's 401(k) plan. You can also complete a roll over yourself by having your employer write you a check, and you can deposit the entire value of your 401(k) into an IRA. However, there are two snags: 1) your company has to withhold 20 percent to cover potential taxes–and you have to fill in this gap when opening the IRA, and 2) all this must be done within 60 days of receipt of a check from your company.

A word of warning about IRA roll over accounts: If you plan to use an IRA account simply to hold funds while joining the 401(k) of a new employer, do not add any of your own contributions to this IRA. According to tax laws, this will make that IRA ineligible to be transferred to a new 401(k) plan because of the tax-deferred status of the account.

Option 4: Simply cash out and walk away with a check. However, before licking your chops over this prospect of a cash infusion, remember that the check you receive will not reflect the true value of your account once you pay all the applicable taxes and the 10 percent early withdrawal penalty. A $10,000 401(k) for example, might yield only $6200 after all taxes and penalties.

Without an incredible amount of effort, an employer-sponsored retirement plan has the ability, through just a little planning and forethought, to allow you to live up to your expectations for retirement. However, the key to being successful is to start early and know the rules of the game. After a little bit of work, just sit back, let the markets do the work, and concentrate on your career.

Individual Retirement Accounts (IRAs)

Another way to save for retirement, whether you have an employer-sponsored plan or not, is through an Individual Retirement Account, also known as an IRA. This type of account, created by Congress in 1974, was originally designed to promote retirement savings, specifically for those who did not have pension coverage from their employers. IRA rules have been changed several times over the past two decades, with the present day IRA stemming from modifications made in 1986.

Each year, as long as you have taxable compensation and have not reached age 70½ by the end of the year, you are permitted to contribute up to $2000, or 100 percent of your salary, whichever is lower, into an IRA. You can do this in addition to your employer's retirement plan. However, depending on a number of factors, your contribution may or may not be tax deductible. Contributions are only fully tax deductible in the two following situations:

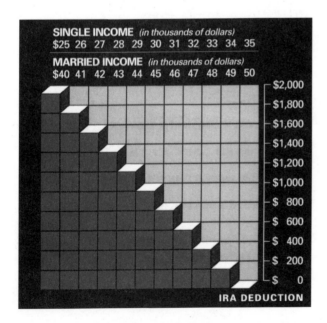

1) You or your spouse are not covered by a company retirement plan.

2) You are covered under a company plan but are single and have an adjusted gross income of less than $25,000, or married and have a joint adjusted gross income of less than $40,000.

In all other circumstances, only part of your contributions will be deductible. At the end of the year, if you have made deductions that are not deductible, you will have to indicate this by filing a Form 8606 with your taxes. Contributions can be made any time during the year up to the due date for filing your tax return for the year. Extensions do not count.

Much like the 401(k) plans described earlier in this chapter, once you open an IRA, whether or not your contributions are deductible, the dividends, interest, and capital gains you earn are allowed to accumulate tax-deferred until withdrawal. This compounding allows your money to accumulate at a much faster rate than it would in a traditional savings account.

How do I get one?

IRAs can be opened at most financial institutions, from banks to mutual fund companies. Most companies that sell IRAs offer a number of different choices into which participants can invest their contributions. By law, IRAs are permitted to be invested in marketable securities such as stock and bonds, interest-bearing accounts, and gold and silver coins issued by the U.S. or a state government. The investment allocation decision is up to you, although the menu may vary, depending on the institution from which you purchase your plan. However, if you are not happy with your choice, IRA assets can be transferred, with some restrictions, from one IRA to another. Among the companies offering special IRA products:

Vanguard: (800) 205-6189

American Century: (800) 345-2021

Fidelity: (800) 544-7272

Strong: (800) 368-1030

Since IRAs are designed to help people save for retirement, the law makes it unpleasant to take money out before you reach the age of 59½. Except in certain circumstances, withdrawals before age 59½ will incur a 10 percent penalty as well as all applicable taxes. There are a few exceptions where this 10 percent penalty is waived:

1) If you become disabled before 59½, the 10 percent penalty is waived.

2) If you die before 59½, the assets of your IRA can be distributed without the 10 percent penalty.

3) Withdrawals in the form of a lifetime annuity.

4) Withdrawals to pay medical expenses in excess of 7.5 percent of your AGI (Adjusted Gross Income).

5) Withdrawals to pay health insurance premiums while unemployed.

You must start withdrawals by April 1 of the year following the year in which you become age 70½.

If you are married, both you and your spouse may contribute up to $2000 each to separate IRAs. If you work and your spouse does not, the law allows you to establish what is known as a Spousal IRA, in which contributions to both you and your spouse's IRA can both equal $2000.

Individual Retirement Accounts provide an excellent way to save tax-deferred money until retirement, especially for people not covered by a retirement plan. Specific details about IRAs are available from the company offering the plan or from Internal Revenue Service Publication 590, which can be ordered by calling (800) 829-3676.

More Chances To Save

Contained in the budget deal agreed upon by Congress and the President in the summer of 1997 are several changes to the law which will benefit individual investors. First off, income limits for individuals to be able to deduct their full contribution to an IRA will be raised by $5000 for single filers and by $10,000 for joint filers in 1998. Gradually, these limits will slowly rise to $50,000 for single filers and $80,000 for joint filers. In addition, a new type of IRA, known as a "Roth IRA" was created which will allow individuals to make after-tax contributions of up to $2000 a year into Roth IRA, and then withdraw the interest and principle tax free. Withdrawals from these accounts cannot occur until the account has been held for at least five years and the accountholder is age 59½, unless the withdraws are used to buy a first home or pay college bills.

Q.u.i.c.k. D.o.w.n.l.o.a.d.

- Retirement may seem like a long way off, but to accumulate the amount of money you will need, it's important to start saving now. The current entitlement programs like Social Security and Medicare that provide income and benefits to senior citizens will probably not be around in their current form for us because of demographic changes that may seriously weaken or bankrupt the system.

- Congress has created two ways for individuals to save for retirement now. They are known as (1) employer-sponsored retirement plans, such as 401(k)s, and (2) Individual Retirement Accounts (IRAs).

- Accounts, such as 401(k)s, allow employees to contribute money tax-deferred. That means the money that goes into the account—as well as the growth of the account itself—is exempt from taxes until some point in the future, usually retirement. The advantage to this is that it decreases an individual's taxable income and enables the investment to compound more quickly.

- Employers have the option to match some or all of the money contributed by the employee.

- The employee does not own the money contributed by the employer to this account until he or she is vested. There are two kinds vesting: Cliff vesting is when you can keep 100 percent of the employer-contributed money at the end of a predetermined length of service, say five years. Graded vesting is when you gradually become vested between a certain number of years. An employee's contributions are always 100 vested.

- Money invested into a 401(k) may go into a number of options, including mutual funds or company stock. It's important to select an investment option that matches your needs and risk tolerance.

- Money contributed to a 401(k) is for long-term use. In general, therefore, any money taken out before age 59 is subject to a 10 percent early with-drawal penalty and all applicable taxes.

- It is possible to access money in a 401(k) for what's known as financial hardship. The tax code recognizes four specific hardships: unreimbursable medical expenses, purchase of a primary residence, payment of post-secondary tuition for you or a dependent for the next year, or to prevent eviction from or foreclosure on your home. Hardship withdrawals are still subject to the 10 percent early withdrawal penalty as well as taxes.

- There are certain circumstances in which you are exempt from the 10 percent early withdrawal penalty. These are severance of service from your company, if over the age of 55, disability, or death.

- An individual may take out a loan against the balance of his or her 401(k) plan. The advantage to doing so is that the interest rate is often below that of the commercial bank, and the interest payments go back to you instead of being lost to a bank or credit union.

- When leaving a job where you've opened a 401(k), there are several options of what to do with the plan. They can include keeping the money in the account where it is, moving the money into the 401(k) of a new company, rolling the funds into an IRA, or cashing out the account altogether. That last option requires that the investor pay an early withdrawal penalty and all applicable taxes.

- IRAs are also tax-deferred accounts that can be opened through banks, mutual funds companies, insurance firms, and other institutions.

- Individuals can make contributions of up to $2000 a year or 100 percent of their salary (whichever is less) to an IRA. These contributions are fully tax deductible in the two following situations: (1) You are not covered by a company retirement plan (2) you are covered under a company plan but are single and have an adjusted gross income of less than $25,000, or married and have a joint adjusted gross income of less than $40,000.

TERMS TO KNOW

American Stock Exchange (AMEX): A trading house in New York where stocks are auctioned between brokers. Small to medium-sized companies as well as a large number of oil and gas companies are traded on this exchange.

Annual Report: An often glossy publication, put out by management, that summarizes the performance of a company or mutual fund over one year (calendar or fiscal) and discusses future prospects; also a public relations device to attract new investors.

Back-End Load: Deferred commission fee ("load") or sales charge that is paid when a mutual fund is sold.

Balanced Fund: A mutual fund that invests in both stocks and bonds—usually with an unbalanced ratio of 60:40.

Bear Market: When stock prices generally fall as a whole. Since World War I, there have been ten major bear markets. Bear markets are usually brought on by fears of declining economic activity.

Beta: A fancy way of evaluating risk (i.e, "volatility") for a particular mutual fund or stock, relative to the market as a whole. A fund with a beta of 1 has the same risk as the market. A beta 2 fund is twice as risky, so that an investor is likely to double his or her profits (or losses!) compared to the market. A beta of less than one means the mutual fund or stock moves comparatively less than the market as a whole.

Blue Chip Stock: Dubbed after the blue chips in poker, the most valuable ones, these are shares in older, established companies, such as IBM, AT&T, and GM, that have a long history of growth dividend distribution. The 30 Dow Jones Industrial Average stocks are all blue chips.

Bond: A formal IOU ("certificate") from a corporation, the U.S. Treasury, or local governments to pay back a debt—with interest—at a specified time ("maturity date"). Unlike stockholders, bondholders own only the debt, not a share of a corporation.

Bond Fund: A mutual fund that invests only in corporate, U.S. Treasury, or local government securities. They provide lower returns and emphasize income over rapid gains or losses.

Bond Rating: A grade given to bonds that indicates the quality of the investment. As in school, the more A's the better, ranging from AAA (very unlikely to default) to D (in default). Moody's Investment Services and Standard & Poor's are the two major bond rating companies.

Broker: A certified person who acts as an intermediary between the individual and the exchange in buying and selling securities, such as stock. Brokers charge a fee, known as a commission, for this service.

Bull Market: When the price of stocks generally rises. Fortunately, stock prices tend to rise over the long term, but as John Maynard Keynes observed, in the long run we're all dead.

Capital: Money; the financial assets you own that can be invested.

Capital Appreciation: The rise in value of a security, such as a stock. If you buy a share of stock for $100 and it increases in value to $125, the capital appreciation is $25.

Capital Gain/Loss: The amount of profit gained–or lost–after selling an investment. Stock bought for $100 and sold for $125 has produced $25 in capital gain. However, that same stock sold for $75 results in a $25 capital loss. Capital gains are taxable income.

Certificate of Deposit (CD): Similar to regular savings accounts, but they pay a higher interest because the length and amount of deposit are locked in, from 14 days to several years. This is the most common type of money market instrument. CDs cashed in before maturity are subject to substantial penalties for early withdrawal.

Closed-End Fund: A mutual fund with a limited number of shares that are bought and sold on the stock exchange or in over-the-counter (OTC) markets. Unlike an open-end fund (where the share price is based on the value of the fund's assets), the price of a closed-end share is determined by supply and demand, just like a stock.

Commercial Paper: Short-term IOUs–from 2 to 270 days–sold by corporations to raise funds.

Commission: A fee paid by an investor to a broker or dealer for an investment transaction or advice. Commissions are charged when a security, such as a stock, is bought or sold.

Common Stock: Securities that show ownership in a corporation. Stockholders share profits or losses in the corporation through dividends and changes in the stock's market value. Common stock is the most prevalent type of stock issued.

Compounding: The process of growth building upon growth in an investment. The result is increased gains on the investment over time.

Consumer Price Index (CPI): The rate of inflation as shown by the change in price of a set group of consumer goods and services tracked by the Bureau of Labor Statistics in Washington.

Convertible Bonds: IOUs ("certificates") that can be exchanged for common stock of the same corporation. Unlike regular bonds that fluctuate in value based upon interest rate, these bonds tend to fluctuate in price based on the price of stock.

Corporation: A business organization with limited liability. The owners, including shareholders, can lose only the amount they invest.

Current Return: How much your original investment grows over one year.

Defined-Contribution Plan: A retirement plan, such as a 401(k), with set employer and/or employee contributions, usually a percentage of salary. The amount of income that an individual is able to withdraw from this kind of plan is based upon contributions, length of service, and earnings.

Discount Broker: Opposite of a full-service broker, these are no-frills investment dealers who provide basic trading services at low cost, including, generally, online trading services. Investors do not receive advice or recommendations when using this kind of broker. Charles Schwab and Quick & Reilly are two examples of discount brokers.

Diversification: Reducing risk by investing in more than one type of security, such as stocks, bonds, and money market devices. Mutual funds provide individuals with instant diversification by investing in many different securites.

Dividend: Cash profits that are distributed to shareholders from net profits of a corporation or mutual fund. It's usually given out quarterly and it's taxable.

Dollar-Cost Averaging: The strategy in which an investor buys the same dollar amount (say $100) of a stock at regular intervals, regardless of the changing price of the stock. Since shares are bought at both high and low prices, this strategy averages those costs out over the long run.

Dow Jones Industrial Average (DJIA): The average cost of 30 of the largest NYSE-listed stocks. It's the most widely quoted indicator of the market's movement, but because it's so narrow (there are about 3000 stocks on the New York Stock Exchange), it doesn't truly portray broad market action.

Dividend Reinvestment Plan (DRIP): An investment arrangement in which corporate dividends, instead of being received as cash by the shareholder, are automatically used to purchase more shares of that firm's stock without paying commissions. DRIPs provide a low-cost way to steadily increase the portfolio value in a particular stock.

Earnings: Also known as profits, they are the amount of money a company clears after paying all applicable expenses.

Federal Deposit Insurance Corporation (FDIC): A public corporation that insures accounts in participating banks up to $100,000 for losses.

Financial Risk: The likelihood that a company will not pay back its investors.

Fixed Income: A guaranteed rate of interest on an investment. Bonds, which pay specific amounts of money over time, are an example of a fixed-income security.

401(k): Employer-sponsored retirement plan that allows employees to defer taxes on a portion of their salaries by contributing to a company investment account, usually into mutual funds.

403(b): Similar to 401(k)s, but for employees of universities, public schools, and nonprofit organizations.

Front-End Load: Up-front commission fee (or "load") investors pay when they buy shares in a fund. Loads are calculated as a percentage, such as 2 or 3 percent, of the amount that an indivdiual invests into a mutual fund. The load on a $500 investment with a 2 percent charge is $10.

Full-Service Broker: An investment dealer who provides a full range of investment advice—usually at higher cost—including research, investment planning, and trading.

Growth Stock: Shares, usually in small companies with potentially bright futures and fast growth.

Income Stock: Shares in companies with a history of paying high dividends but lacking fast growth. Utility companies, such as gas and electric firms, with a constant customer base and income flow are some of the best-known income stocks.

Index: A way to measure market performance as a whole based on a set of stocks, such as the Dow Jones Industrial Average or the Standard and Poor's 500.

Index Fund: A mutual fund that strictly invests in shares of a particular stock index, such as the Standard and Poor's 500 or Russell 2000. These funds generally have low costs and fees.

Individual Retirement Account (IRA): A special savings account that allows individuals to contribute money for retirement without paying taxes on either the money that is added or the interest that is generated. In general, money from IRAs cannot be removed until age $59^{1/2}$ without paying a 10 percent penalty.

Inflation: The declining value of money due to rising prices. When stuff costs more, your money buys less and less.

Inflation-Indexed Bonds: U.S. Treasury IOUs ("certificates") pegged to the inflation rate. The value of the bond increases at the same pace as inflation.

Initial Public Offering (IPO): When a private company goes "public" by selling shares for the first time.

Interest: The price paid for the use of money. A lender earns interest; a borrower pays interest.

Investing: Putting money into securities like stocks, bonds, or mutual funds with the hope that it will grow in value.

Investment: Wherever you put your money (stocks, bonds, mutual funds, real estate) with the expectation that it will increase in value.

Investment Grade: Bonds with moderate to low risk, usually with a BBB rating or above.

Investment Objective: Broad goals of a mutual fund or other investment. In general, portfolios seek income (blue chip), capital appreciation (growth stock), safety (bonds), or some combination of these three.

Junk Bonds: IOUs from companies that already have high debt and are therefore more likely to not pay the IOU back. They offer high interest rates and high risk.

Keogh Plan: A tax-deferred retirement plan for self-employed people and small businesses.

Liquidity: A measure of how easily an investment can be converted to cash. Cash is 100 percent liquid. All other savings and investment options are liquid to a lesser degree than cash.

Load: A sales charge paid shareholders of mutual funds when buying or selling a mutual fund. In general, low-load funds charge 1 to 3 percent, medium-loads, 3 to 6 percent, and full-load, 6 to 8.5 percent, while no-load funds don't charge any load.

Market Capitalization: The amount of stock a corporation is allowed to issue or has already sold.

Market Risk: Fluctuations in prices for the market as a whole or in specific sectors, brought on by outside forces. For example, crude oil prices increased drastically in 1990 because of the Iraqi invasion of Kuwait.

Maturity Date: Nothing to do with puberty, but rather the day when an IOU (such as a bond or certificate of deposit) must be repaid to the lender.

Minimum Distribution: The amount that an investor's retirement plan must pay when she or he reaches 70 years.

Money Market Account: Accounts opened at financial institutions where the money is invested into safe, short-term debt instruments, such as CDs and U.S. Treasury bills. They usually pay a higher return than regular savings accounts.

Money Market Fund: A mutual fund that invests primarily in relatively safe, short term debt instruments (IOUs). The price for one share of these funds is typically $1.

Municipal Bond: IOUs ("certificates") sold by state and local governments to investors. Usually, the interest earned is exempt from taxes.

Mutual Fund: An investment company that pools money of individuals and invests it into stocks, bonds, and other securities under the guidance of a professional manager. A mutual fund offers shareholders the benefits of portfolio diversification—owning a wide set of shares to spread risk, gains, and losses.

NASDAQ: Stands for the National Association of Securities Dealers Automated Quotations. In reality, it's the computerized system for brokers and dealers to trade shares in companies in the over-the-counter market. No actual trading floor exists; all price quotes and stocks are exchanged electronically. Smaller and newer companies are typically traded on NASDAQ, and most technology stocks, such as Microsoft and Intel.

Net Asset Value (NAV): The price of one share of a mutual fund, calculated by adding the total investments in a fund, subtracting costs, and dividing by the total number of shares. Net asset value (N-A-V, not "nav-h") is a key indicator on your investment and is usually given in newspaper listings of mutual fund performance.

New Issues: The first public sale of an investment instrument (stocks or bonds) by a company.

New York Stock Exchange (NYSE): Located on Wall Street in Manhattan and known as the "Big Board," it's the largest and oldest trading house for stocks in the world. Shares in older, established companies are bought and sold on the NYSE.

No-Load Mutual Fund: A mutual fund that does not impose a sales charge, or load, when it's bought or sold by the investor.

Odd Lot: When you buy fewer than 100 shares of a company's stock at one time. Brokers may charge additional commission fees for buying or selling odd lots.

Open-End Fund: A mutual fund that is willing to sell more shares—and also buy shares back from investors—to meet demand and to increase its pool of money available to invest. Most mutual funds on the market today are open-end funds.

Penny Stock: Very low-priced, high-risk, speculative shares in unproven companies. Many technology companies are considered penny stocks.

Portfolio: The various investments owned by an individual or mutual fund, such as stocks, bonds, and money market accounts.

Preferred Stock: A type of stock that gets first dibs on dividends and money—before common stock—if the corporation goes bust. These stocks tend not to fluctuate as greatly in price as common stocks in the same firm would.

Price/Earnings (P/E) Ratio: The price of a share of stock divided by the last 12 months of its profits. This ratio reflects how much investors are willing to pay for a share's earning power. The P/E ratio is calculated by taking the price that a share of stock is trading at and dividing by the earnings per share of that firm (that's the total profits of the company divided by the number of shares it has outstanding). It's used as a gauge to find out how high or low a stock is trading compared to its real earning's potential.

Principal: The amount of money originally invested.

Prospectus: Document that describes a mutual fund's investment objectives, policies, fees, and the like. The law requires that you read the prospectus for a mutual fund—or at least acknowledge to have read it—prior to investing in any fund.

Proxy: Written authorization giving someone else your right to vote at a shareholders' meeting. Often used by shareholders who simply are unable, or do not wish to attend a shareholders' meeting.

Rate of Return: How much money you get back for your investment. For stocks, it's the annual dividends divided by the purchase price. For bonds, it's the actual amount of interest earned.

Real Estate: Property consisting of land and all permanently attached structures and buildings, such as houses or apartments.

Risk: Uncertainty as to whether or not an investment choice will perform as expected, particularly due to factors beyond one's control (in other words, the odds an investment will make or lose money).

Risk/Reward: The tension between preserving your investment and maximizing your profit. In general, the higher the return, the more likely you are to lose your initial investment. Lower risk usually results in less profit.

Rollover: Shifting retirement savings from one qualified fund to another without having to pay a tax penalty.

Securities: The generic term for stocks, bonds, and money market investments.

Securities and Exchange Commission (SEC): The federal regulatory board that oversees stock and bond trading—and mutual funds—to help ensure that investors don't get ripped off. Founded after the Great Crash in 1929 to keep it from happening again.

Share: A unit sold to an investor that represents a measure of ownership ("equity") in a corporation or mutual fund.

Social Security: A government insurance program that provides income and health benefits to retirees and others. Benefits paid are based on the contribution an individual makes during his or her lifetime.

Standard & Poor's Rating: A grade assigned to a bond that represents the likelihood the debt will be paid back. Ratings of BBB to AAA are called "investment grade" because they are low-risk investments. Anything below that is more risky.

Stock: A security that represents partial ownership in a corporation. The value of a stock generally reflects the financial performance of a company.

Stock Certificate: The document giving legal ownership of a specific number of shares in a corporation.

Stockholder: An individual investor in a corporation.

Stock Split: Dividing the total stock of a company into proportionately more shares in order to bring the price down and make the stock more marketable. If a stock splits 2-for-1, for instance, an investor owning 40 shares would get 80, but the price per share would drop by half to maintain the same portfolio value.

Street Name: When investments are held in the name of a broker rather than the name of the investor.

Taxable Income: The amount of money you earn (including interest, stock sales, etc.) that you have to pay federal and state taxes on.

Tax Deferred: The right to put off paying federal taxes on your investments until much later down the road.

Total Return: The percentage of total profits earned on an initial investment over a period of time. For mutual funds, it's usually reported in newspapers for the current year-to-date, twelve months, and three or five years.

Treasury Bills (T-Bills): Low-risk, low-income debt (IOUs, usually sold in $10,000 increments) of one year or less issued by the U.S. Treasury Department to cover costs. No interest is paid, but the debt is sold at less than face value and repaid for full value when it comes due.

Treasury Bonds: Similar to Treasury bills, but the debt (IOU) is sold in $1000 denominations and is repaid between seven and thirty years, with fixed interest on the debt paid every six months.

Treasury Notes: Similar to Treasury bonds but with maturities of one to seven years.

12b-1 Fee: Different and often in addition to loads, this is an annual mutual fund sales charge levied on investments for promotion and marketing costs in the fund. It's named for the Securities and Exchange Commission rule that allows funds to charge the fee.

U.S. Savings Bonds: Registered, nontransferable IOUs ("certificates") sold by the federal government with a variety of interest and maturity dates as specified by the type ("series") of debt sold. These are the types of bonds you received as a gift back as a youngster.

Venture Capital: Money invested in a start-up company by an outsider in the hope of making big profits—generally when the company goes public.

Vesting: When an employee becomes eligible for retirement benefits from the employer, whether the employee remains with the company or not. *Cliff vesting* is when you can keep 100 percent of the employer contributed money at the end of a predetermined length of service, such as five years. *Graded vesting* is when you gradually become vested between a certain number of years. For instance, you may become vested 20 percent each year between your second and seventh years until you eventually reach 100 percent.

Yield: The amount of money you get from your investment, stated as a percentage of the original investment.

Zero Coupon Bond: An IOU ("certificate") that sells for much less than its stated value. Though no interest is paid, the debt gradually increases in value until it is paid back at full value.

Index